Garden Furniture
& Features

Garden Furniture
& Features

From Benches and Gazebos to Sundials and Treehouses

ALEX WARD & NICK GIBBS

APPLE

A QUARTO BOOK

First published in the United Kingdom
by Apple Press
Sheridan House, 112–116a Western Road
Hove, East Sussex BN3 1DD

www.apple-press.com

ISBN 1-84092-424-1

QUAR.BIGA

Conceived, designed and produced by
Quarto Publishing plc
The Old Brewery
6 Blundell Street
London N7 9BH

Senior project editors: Kate Tuckett and Claire Wedderburn-Maxwell
Senior art editor: Sally Bond
Designer: Andrew Easton @ Talking Design
Text editor: Stuart Cooper
Photographer: Paul Forrester
Illustrators: Kuo Kang Chen, John Woodcock, Sally Bond

Art director: Moira Clinch
Publisher: Piers Spence

Colour separation by Universal Graphics Pte Ltd, Singapore
Printed in China by SNP Leefung Printers Limited

NOTE TO OUR READERS
All do-it-yourself activities involve a degree of risk. Skills, materials,
tools and site conditions vary widely. Although the editors have made
every effort to ensure accuracy, the reader remains responsible for the
selection and use of tools, materials and methods. Always obey local
codes and laws, follow manufacturer's operating instructions and
observe safety precautions.

1 3 5 7 9 10 8 6 4 2

Contents

Introduction

Gardening gives you the opportunity to create an outdoor space of your own. In addition to being practical, building garden furniture and other structures expresses your creativity and lets you extend your home's décor and style to the yard and garden.

◀ A tuteur, or free-standing trellis, is an ideal structure on which to grow favorite climbing plants.

Twenty practical projects form the heart of this book. Thanks to the easy designs, even a beginner woodworker who owns a few tools can succeed with these plans. Plus, all of the projects are made with readily available materials. Additional pages of inspiration show accessories you can buy to enhance your outdoor living space.

To begin, you'll need only a few tools. However, we've used these projects as a way to introduce you to more specialized equipment. If you do have some woodworking experience, you will see the potential for modifying our designs and building them with alternative materials and equipment.

We've started with an introduction to the tools, techniques and materials you'll need. We explain, in a clear step-by-step format, the procedures you'll use. We also highlight solutions to common problems and give you useful tips and suggestions.

▲ This practical as well as attractive nautically themed weather vane will suit most garden schemes.

In the Inspiration and Projects section, commercially available products mentioned may inspire you to create your own furniture. If you don't have time to do any building right now, they will give you ideas about what to purchase. We also include information to help you get more enjoyment from your yard.

"Pots and Planters," page 30, gives directions on how to make a classic planter, a stylish planter bench

◄ The clever design of this portable bench means that you can move it around the garden—into the shade or sun—to suit your mood.

▲ Delightfully strong yet elegant, this chair is designed to complement any garden.

and a raised planter that can also double as a water feature. Charts list the characteristics of the materials you can use for planters and detail the plants that grow especially well in containers.

Most people use their garden as an extra room these days, so the largest section of the book is dedicated to "Sitting and Eating," page 52. Projects in this chapter include a number of stylish chairs, benches and tables, including a Mosaic Table and a Wheelbarrow Bench, plus ideas for tantalizing accessories.

If you aren't already using your garden as a series of outdoor rooms, turn to "Divisions and Doorways," page 100, for inspiration. Create trellis screens and arches to define private spaces or tuteurs on which to grow climbing plants.

A garden isn't a garden without some wildlife. Whether you live in a city, town, the suburbs or in a rural area, "Wildlife Winners," page 126, overflows with information to help you attract birds to your garden and protect them from predators. You'll find projects for building a birdhouse, a bird feeder and even a dovecote.

Finally, in "Leisure," page 144, plans for fantastic structures, a fort for children, as well as a swing bench and hammock support, suggest projects for fun and relaxation. The weather vane will also delight both young and old visitors to your garden.

Even if a project seems daunting at first, don't let that intimidate you. The instruction and guidance provided for each project will help you create something that you and your family can enjoy for many years to come.

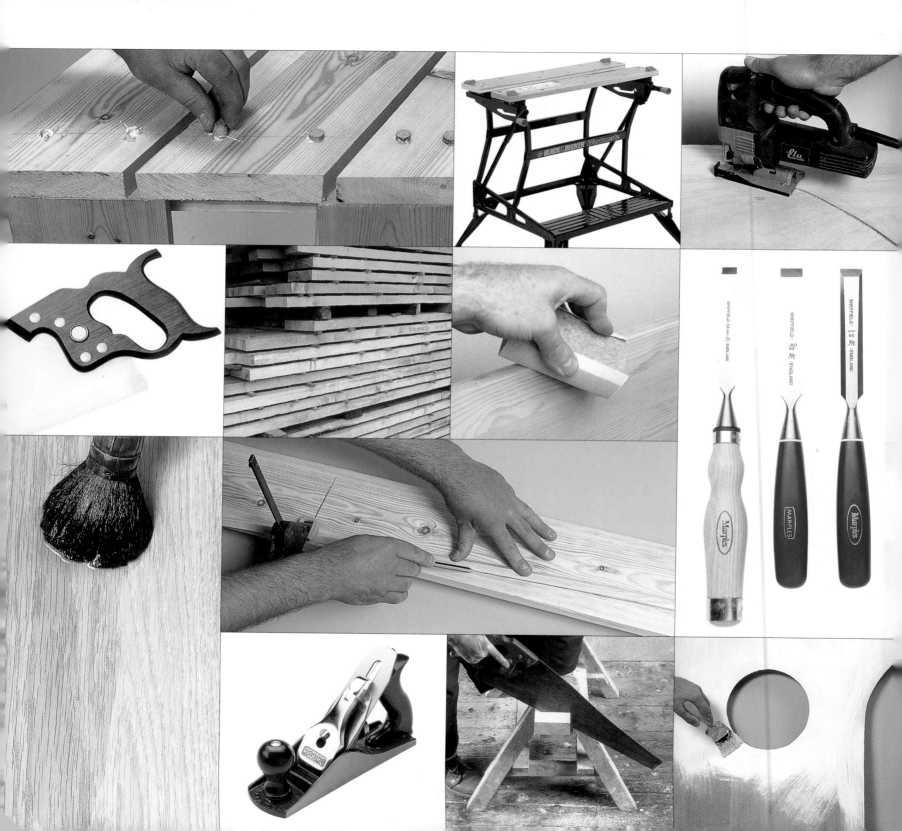

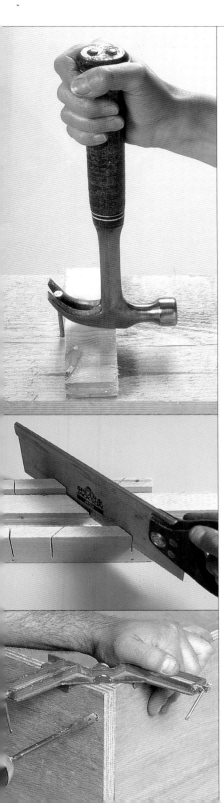

TOOLS, TECHNIQUES AND FINISHES

The projects in this book all require basic woodworking skills and relatively simple tools to cut, drill and assemble the pieces of each project together. In fact, you probably already own most of the tools featured here and know all the basic techniques.

You will need only a few tools to start making your own garden furniture. If you are a beginner, some projects may introduce you to more specialized equipment. If you do have some woodworking experience already, you will see the potential for modifying our designs and building them with alternative materials and equipment to create your own unique furniture.

We've started with an introduction to the tools, techniques and materials you'll need and then clearly explain the procedures you'll use. We highlight solutions to common problems and give you tips and suggestions so that you can make a wide range of furniture with confidence.

Tools

The projects are made from plywood and softwood to keep construction as simple as possible. All of them make use of easy to find dimensional lumber. You'll need only a small toolbox to cut, drill and put the pieces of each project together and may already have the tools required. Below we describe commonly used items.

The tools shown here would make an excellent starter set for anyone wanting to get into woodworking on a serious scale: the power tools, in particular, save time and make many procedures much easier. Most operations, however, can be carried out just as well by hand, albeit more slowly.

After each listing we indicate, where applicable, the next tool you might want to acquire to further your hobby.

1. Multipurpose handsaw

Choose a handsaw with a medium cut—one with about 7 medium-long teeth to the inch (25mm)—for the best finish when cutting softwood.

Next purchase: **Tenon or back saw (1.1)** Tenon saws usually have finer teeth than handsaws, as well as reinforced backs for increased accuracy when cutting.

2. Coping saw

Coping saws are used for intricate work, such as cutting tight curves or decorative patterns. Their thin blades may have up to 30 teeth to the inch (25mm).

3. Jigsaw Just as it's worth investing in a good cordless drill, don't skimp on a jigsaw—it will be a loyal friend for many years. Quality jigsaws are much easier to use than inexpensive

models. They have more power, a better sole and greater flexibility. They are ideal for cutting shapes and working with sheet materials because they reduce tearing when cutting across the grain. If you plan to cut a lot of curves, buy a scrolling jigsaw or scrollsaw, which has a pivoting action that makes these cuts easy to do. Always wear goggles and ear protection when using a jigsaw, and use a dust mask to avoid inhaling harmful particles of airborne sawdust.

Next purchase: **A circular saw (3.1) or band saw (3.2)** If you plan to cut a lot of sheet material, buy a hand-held circular saw. Used against a straightedge it improves accuracy and speed. If you plan to make furniture from solid wood, then a small band saw—a hugely versatile tool for cutting all kinds of shapes—is the tool you'll need.

4.1

5

6

7.2

7

7.1

7.3

4. Miter saw Although you can mark and cut wood to length at 90 degrees, 45 degrees or any other angle by either eye using a handsaw or using a miter box for guidance, your best bet is to buy a miter saw, sometimes called a chop saw. Miter saws are held in a movable frame and the wood is positioned against a fence. These saws are inexpensive and rapidly pay for themselves. They give a better finish and assure greater accuracy for miter joints—which are much more difficult to cut than you might imagine!

Next purchase: **A table saw with sliding cross-cut fence or a radial arm saw (4.1)** Either of these entails a substantial investment in machinery, but they open whole new horizons in woodworking. As an alternative, buy a band saw for cutting boards roughly to length and combine it with a stationary disk sander to adjust miters accurately.

5. Portable workbench
Being able to hold wood securely when cutting, drilling and joining it can make the difference between success and failure. You don't need the most expensive model, because some of the lighter, more simple designs with crossed legs are just as good. These may not have as wide a work surface, but they are easier to maneuver and store. They also lack vise components, but having these can be frustrating as they can easily drop out and get lost.

Next purchase: **A couple of inexpensive plastic sawhorses**
These will give you a surface to work on when you are cutting plywood and they also fold up flat. You can

hang them on a wall to keep them out of the way.

6. Cordless drill/driver You'll need a drill for many of the projects in this book, both for drilling and screwing. Look for a cordless drill with good balance—the best drills usually have a central handle. You'll also need some drivers. Look for a set with various sizes of Phillips-head drivers. To make your life even easier, buy a magnetic sleeve to hold the driver in place. You'll soon learn that a drill can be a constant friend in your garage, shed, workshop and around the house.

Next purchase: **Drill press** For accurate drilling, especially where repetitive work is concerned, nothing beats a drill press, which holds the workpiece steady while you lower the drillpoint onto it. Buying an inexpensive model with a small motor is better value than using an electric drill on a stand.

7. Drill bits (7), countersink (7.1) and spade bits (7.2) Many drills come with a few bits included. Whether yours does or not, it's always worth buying a small set of about 10 drill bits ranging from ¹⁄₁₆ inch (2mm) to ⅜ inch (10mm). You'll also need a countersink and a few spade bits— ⅜ inch (10mm) and ¾ inch (19mm) should do. The smaller spade bit can double as a countersink.

Next purchase: **More drill bits (7.3)**
Bits that combine a countersink or counterbore are particularly useful. You may also want to buy a plug cutter to make your own wooden plugs to hide screw heads, but you will need a drill press to use it.

BASIC TOOL KIT
Each project in this book contains a list of all of the materials and equipment you will need. When we refer to a basic tool kit, we mean the 14 main items listed on these pages. Any additional equipment that is needed is itemized separately for each project.

8. Combination square This tool combines a ruler, a straightedge and often a spirit level, and has 90 degree and 45 degree settings. It's worth paying for a quality model as a cheap one will rarely be accurate.

Checking for accuracy: Before you use the combination square, first check for accuracy by marking a line across a board at 90 degrees. Then flip the square around and do the same thing with the fence pointing in the other direction. Draw a line very close to the first one. If the lines are parallel, the square is fine. If not, the square needs adjusting or replacement.

Next purchase: **Bevel square (8.1)** Once you get into serious woodworking, you'll want a more accurate square, particularly to mark more complicated joints. A sliding bevel, sometimes called an angle finder, allows you to find and mark any angle, for example, determining the pitch of a roof.

9. Steel tape measure A retractable steel tape measure is essential for any woodworker. Buy a good-quality tape—cheap ones have weak springs and weak holding pieces at the end.

Next purchase: **Another tape**, for the moment you misplace your first!

10. Hammer and nail set The projects call for a fair amount of nailing, although in some instances you may prefer to use screws. Screws are more expensive than nails but are more secure and easier to use. If you do use nails, you will need a nail set to sink the nail heads below the surface of the wood.

11. Block plane Nothing beats a block plane for beveling the ends of legs and chamfering or rounding edges. Choose one with a screw adjustment because it makes it far easier to get the blade setting right. Block planes are very light and the low angle of the blade handles awkward grains well.

Next purchase: **Smoothing plane (11.1)** For serious hand planing you'll need something longer and heavier than a block plane. Don't buy a hand-held power planer unless you need to plane lots of old boards that could damage your plane irons or you expect to do a lot of home renovation and need to adjust pieces to fit.

12. Sandpaper and block A good selection of coarse, medium and fine grade sandpapers, together with a piece of softwood to wrap them around, are an essential part of any tool kit. Ergonomically shaped cork blocks that fit into your hand are even better—they are more comfortable than wooden blocks. Some have pins to hold the sandpaper.

Next purchase: **Random orbit sander (12.1)** These hand-held power sanders combine the spinning action of a disk sander and the swirling action of the orbital type. They sand quite quickly and don't leave many marks behind, so they are ideal for finishing projects around the home.

13. Chisel In these projects you'll use a chisel for cleaning out corners between saw cuts. You need only one to start with, a ⅝ inch (15mm) bevel-edged type,

12.1

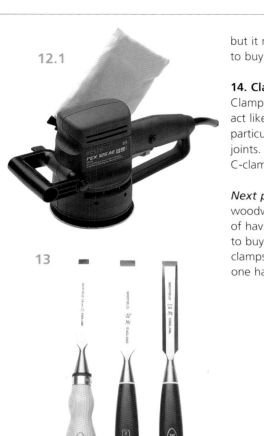

but it makes better economic sense to buy a set.

14. Clamps

Clamps are very handy because they act like a pair of extra hands and are particularly useful when making joints. Start with two 6 inch (150mm) C-clamps.

Next purchase: **More clamps** No woodworker has ever complained of having too many clamps! It is best to buy either "fast clamps," or clamps that you can use with just one hand.

13

14

SHARPENING TOOLS

There's no better way to get to know a tool than by sharpening it as soon as you take it out of the box. Most people are tempted to start planing or chiseling right away, of course, and to keep using a tool until it loses its edge. By that time, however, you might have forgotten what the edge looked like. So buy a combination oilstone with fine and medium grade sides, and a honing guide to help you keep the blade of the plane or chisel at the correct angle.
Notice that there's a difference of about 5 degrees between the angle of the main bevel and the short bevel at the edge of the plane blades. This means that you don't have to work on the whole bevel every time you want to sharpen the blade. However, remember to smooth the back of the blade as well as the bevel. You'll soon be an expert and sharpening will no longer feel like a chore.

Combination oilstone

Diamond stone

Using a honing guide

STORING TOOLS

Buy yourself a simple toolbox to keep your tools neat, clean and in good condition. A toolbox is particularly valuable if you don't yet have a dedicated woodworking area and your tools tend to drift around the house. A tool roll helps to store chisels and screwdrivers, so it's also a good investment.

Hold chisel at correct angle

Key Techniques

You don't need advanced carpentry skills to make these projects. In fact they are designed so that anyone with a few tools can make them relatively quickly. Joining pieces of lumber is a key part of serious woodworking, and the prospect of having to cut complex joints puts many people off this rewarding activity. So we've gone out of our way to make the joints simple—most require no more than glue and nails or screws.

CUTTING TO LENGTH

Many projects require cutting a group of wooden slats to length. This is called crosscutting, and you can do it with a multipurpose handsaw, a tenon saw, or a circular saw. You will need to rest the wood on a sawhorse or workbench as you cut.

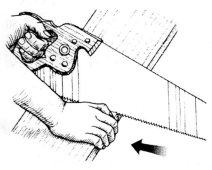

1 Start the cut at the far edge of the wood, with your knee on the board to hold it. This is faster than using a clamp to hold the wood in place. Using your thumb as a guide for the saw and always cutting to the waste side of the marking guide initially, make short strokes toward yourself. Do not put pressure on the saw while making these initial strokes—use them to ease into the cut.

2 As you progress, raise the saw handle and use a full stroke length to make the cut. Let the saw do the work. Extend your forefinger down the handle to keep your arm straight. At first you may not be cutting vertically, but you'll soon find the right position to do so.

3 As you move across the board, lower the handle of the saw so that the teeth start cutting across the top of the board. As always, work on the outside—toward the scrap area—of the marking line.

USING TEMPLATES

Once you have cut one slat to length, use it as a template to mark the rest. If you use more than one template, there is a risk that the slats will gradually become longer and longer (or shorter and shorter).

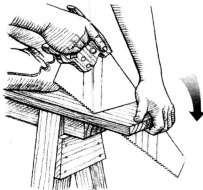

4 As you reach the end of the cut, the waste will begin falling away. At this stage, the risk is that the weight of the waste will tear the last bit of wood before you cut through it. Support the waste end with the hand that isn't holding the saw and make lighter strokes until you feel the waste drop away.

CUTTING A CURVE

The simplest way to cut a curve is with a jigsaw. It's very difficult to cut an accurate curve with any sort of handsaw without a great deal of practice. Clamp a flexible piece of wood loosely along the length of the piece to be cut, bend in to the desired shape, and mark along the curve.

1 Hold the piece of wood on a sawhorse or workbench and start cutting the curve, keeping to the waste side of the line. Put your knee on the board, over the waste side, to prevent it from shifting.

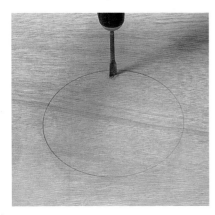

2 To cut out a circular hole, first drill a hole in the waste portion of the circle large enough to get the jigsaw blade through. Insert the blade and cut carefully up to the inside of the line. Proceed to cut the remainder of the circle with care.

RIPPING BOARDS

Cutting with the grain of wood is known as ripping. This is much harder to do than cutting across the grain, because the wood fibers are longer and tend to clog in the cut. This can be done using a multipurpose handsaw, but the task is slow and laborious. It's better to use a circular saw, or best of all, a table saw. Keep the saw straight by clamping a piece of wood to the board to be ripped as a guide, or by using the guide fence on the saw.

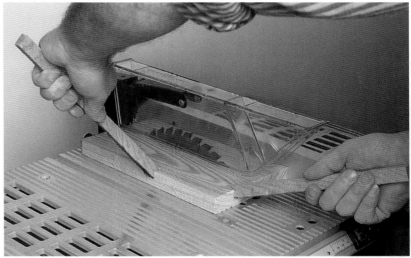

To rip with a table saw, first adjust the rip fence into position and tighten it before the power is switched on. Set the depth of cut to just deeper than the thickness of board to be ripped. The riving knife is there to prevent the wood from closing in and jamming the saw cut as the wood passes through. Use push sticks (easily cut from scrap wood) to guide the wood along the fence and past the blade.

CUTTING GROOVES

As well as ripping and crosscutting, the table saw can be used to cut grooves using the rip fence as a guide. Grooves are widened by adjusting the rip fence after each cut. This is particularly useful for cutting the cheeks of tenons. Grooved or rabbeted cuts can be achieved by using the miter fence with the wood lying the other way.

PLANING WOOD SQUARE

There will be times when you need to plane wood, either because you don't have the right dimensions, the boards are cupped or the faces are not square to the edges. Do this by planing with a smoothing plane. This tool is longer than a block plane, so it gives you more power and greater opportunity to even out bumps and hollows.

1 Choose the best side of the board and hold it against a stop or one of the ears on a workbench. If the ears are too high and might interfere with the plane, clamp a thinner piece of wood across the work surface and plane against this. Do not hold the piece in the jaws of a vise if it is wider than 2 inches (50mm) because the pressure can distort the surface of the wood and it is likely to spring back after you've planed it.

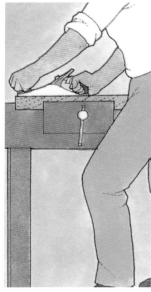

2 As you start planing, apply pressure to the front of the plane. Try to feel the sole of the plane sitting flat on the board. Apply even pressure and start to plane.

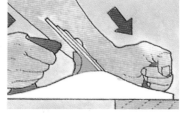

3 As you plane along the board, press toward the back of the plane—this helps to prevent the blade from dipping at the end of the cut. Do not lift the plane until the blade is beyond the wood. Always lift the plane between cuts rather than running the sole back and forth along the wood, which is the most tempting thing to do.

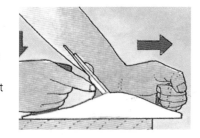

4 To plane the first edge square to the face, hold the wood in a vise. Be certain to keep the center of the plane on the center of the wood. Start with the blade protruding only a very little, cutting a fine shaving to test the grain direction. If the cut is too heavy, you can tear the fibers badly if you are working against the grain.

5 Once you're happy with the cut, adjust the blade to remove more stock, closing it up again for the final finishing passes. Regularly check that the face and edge are square along the whole length. Sometimes it helps to hold the wood up to a light and use a square to check for a gap between the edge and the square.

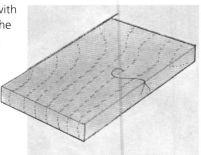

6 Mark a "V" on the best edge with a soft pencil, pointing toward the best face. On the best face, mark a curly symbol that meets the "V." This provides you with the reference for all other work.

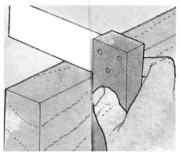

7 To make a board narrower, use a marking gauge to set the width and score a line. Do the same on the other side of the board. Then saw and plane, or if the adjustment is small enough, just plane the board to width.

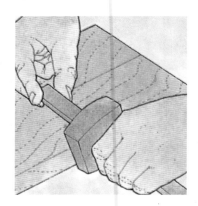

ADJUSTING A PLANE

The best way to get used to your plane is to strip it down to its basic parts and see how they all work in relation to each other. You will then feel confident if you need to adjust it. For best results the plane should be well tuned and adjusted at all times.

1 Make sure the blades on your planes are parallel to the mouth by looking down the sole of the plane from above.

2 Look down the plane from the front to see how much of the blade is showing and to check if it needs lateral adjustment.

MARKING A BOARD TO CUT

To cut to length accurately, use a set square or combination square around all four sides of the piece.

1 Press the stock of the square firmly against the best edge of the board and carefully score a line across the best face of the board.

2 Repeat this process all the way around the board. Shade the waste side or mark it with squiggly lines or an X so you'll know which part is the waste side.

NAILING

Nails are not the strongest way to join wooden parts. You must reinforce the joint with glue, clamp it and leave it long enough to set, which normally means overnight. Nails tend to be better for thinner stock and for moldings, which don't need too much strength and are often too small for screws. Nails can also easily split the wood, but this can be avoided by blunting the tip of the nail with a hammer so that it forces its way through the fibers rather than splitting them. A pilot hole, narrower than the nail, can also help.

1 When hammering a nail into a delicate piece of wood, tap gently until you can feel that it has penetrated the wood.

2 Sink nailheads below the surface with a nail set to give a professional appearance.

ANGLED NAILING

You can make a nailed joint stronger by nailing at a slight angle. This reduces the risk of shearing because the nail will cover more of the wood if it is slightly angled.

3 From time to time, a nail won't go in straight, so you will have to pull it out. To do so, place a piece of scrap on the wood surface, between the wood and the claw end of your hammer. This protects the wood and also gives you more leverage as you pull out the nail.

SANDING

Whenever you sand boards by hand, wrap the sandpaper around a cork or wood block. This keeps it flat and reduces the chance of making dips.

1 Sand in stages, beginning with a coarse (80 to 100 grit) sandpaper, then 120 grit and finally 180 grit sandpaper. Stepping up grades between sandings allows you to remove scratches on the surface—the higher the grade, the smoother the finish. Always sand with the grain to prevent scratching.

2 Woodworkers sometimes refer to removing the arris once a piece is nearly done. What they mean is dulling, or chamfering, the sharp corners of the wood. You can do this by making one or two passes over a corner with very fine (220 grit) sandpaper and a block. Doing this gives a more professional look to a piece, reduces the chance that the wood will splinter and lengthens the life of a paint job because paint adheres better to a rounded edge.

SANDING TIPS

Scratches are often created by rubbing dust particles into the wood with the abrasive, so always brush residue away as you go. Denibbing, when you use very fine sandpaper between coats of finish, is important to remove tiny pimples and produce a perfectly smooth result. After denibbing, collect the particles by wiping the surface with a damp cloth.

If you want to round the edge further, you could use a cornering tool, an item available from specialty woodworking suppliers.

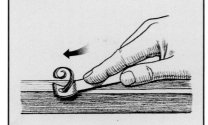

DRILLING

The most important thing when drilling is to hold the drill bit perpendicular to the surface to be drilled at all times. You angle a hole for some types of joints, but for the most part, you don't. A straight hole generally makes the most secure joint. Some of the projects require you to use countersinking bits and spade bits. These bits are more aggressive than standard bits, so it's best to secure the wood with a vise or a specialized workbench.

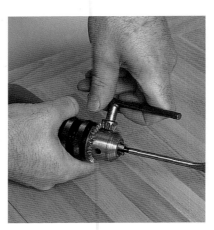

1 Use the chuck key in all three holes when you are using any of the larger bits as it helps to secure them tightly. A secure hold is crucial because these bits loosen more easily than smaller ones. Mark a cross where you want to make the hole and drill where the lines intersect. If you are drilling into very hard wood, drill a small pilot hole first with a very narrow bit. Increase the bit size and the hole by drilling a second time with a larger bit. This technique is important because it allows you to keep the drill precisely where you want it.

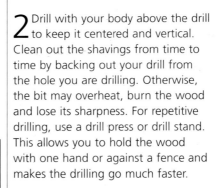

2 Drill with your body above the drill to keep it centered and vertical. Clean out the shavings from time to time by backing out your drill from the hole you are drilling. Otherwise, the bit may overheat, burn the wood and lose its sharpness. For repetitive drilling, use a drill press or drill stand. This allows you to hold the wood with one hand or against a fence and makes the drilling go much faster.

3 To prevent a spade bit from tearing a board as it exits the hole, stop drilling the moment the very tip of the bit breaks through the board. Turn the board over and drill from the other side. This technique also reduces splitting.

BETTER COUNTERSINKING

The most effective way to countersink a screw beneath the surface is to use a countersinking or combination "bit and bore" bit. These bits simultaneously drill a pilot hole and a countersinking hole. They come in various sizes; choose one that is appropriate to the size of the screws you are using. You can also drill for countersinking in two steps with two appropriately sized bits. Begin by drilling through the board to make an appropriately sized pilot hole for the screw. Follow by drilling with a slightly larger bit, sized for the diameter of the plugs you will be using, but this time, drill deeply enough for only the plug—usually about a third of the way through the board, for the projects in this book, about ⅜ inches (10mm) deep.

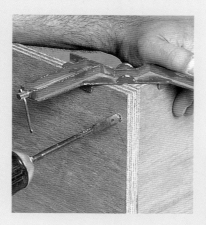

PLUGGING HOLES

To hide a screw head, use a countersinking bit that simultaneously drills a pilot hole and countersinking hole, as described above. Look in a hardware store to find appropriate plugs to fill the countersinking holes; they come in various sizes and colors. If necessary, you can also make your own with a plug cutter.

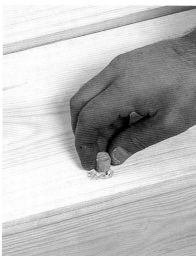

CUTTING SHEET MATERIALS

Sheet materials, such as plywood or particleboard, are large and difficult to maneuver. Fortunately, most home stores and lumberyards will make a couple of cuts free of charge so it is easier to get it home. You can also pay the supplier to make all the cuts you'll need. If you choose to cut up sheet material at home, first place the material on a pair of heavy sawhorses or on 4 x 4s that you've set on a level part of the driveway or yard. Using a jigsaw or circular saw, make only the first cuts with the material on the joists or sawhorses, because this can be awkward. Be careful not to cut through the supports, either. As soon as you have manageable pieces, move the material to a workbench where you can clamp it while you cut.

1 To trim a piece of plywood or other sheet material to size or to cut a thin strip from it, use the fence that comes with the saw. The fence lets you make parallel cuts.

2 To divide a large piece into smaller parts, clamp a straight-edge of a length of wood to the sheet material to use as a guide to cut against. Remember to account for the thickness of the saw blade, or the kerf, when you position the guide as well as the distance between the actual blade and the edge of the saw's table.

3 When you cut plywood, you risk tearing the bottom face. But you can eliminate this problem by using a plywood blade.

CUTTING MITERS

Mitered joints look simple—boards cut at 45 degree angles that are joined together to form 90 degree angles. Although they are simple to cut in principle, many novices find them hard to do accurately. The joints are extremely visible, so you can see any mistakes. Cut boards for these joints very carefully and check that they are meeting correctly as you go.

4 To make internal cuts in plywood or sheet materials, you have to drill some pilot holes into the material so you can position the jigsaw blade where you want to make the cuts. Drill holes into each corner of the cut you'll be making and join them to make the cut. You can now either cut straight lines or curves with the jigsaw. After you make the cuts, sand any rough edges.

1 Mark the wood to be cut to the appropriate angle. Depending on how many sides you are assembling, it will be either 45 or 60 degrees. For four sides, the boards are cut at a 45 degree angle and for six sides, the angle is 60 degrees.

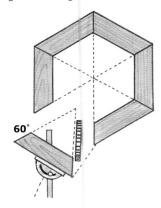

PARING WITH A CHISEL

From time to time, you will need to clean up the surface of a joint or remove a lot of waste. Chisels are good for both of these operations. A ¾ inch (18mm) bevel-edge chisel is the ideal all-purpose tool for the job because it gives you good control and power.

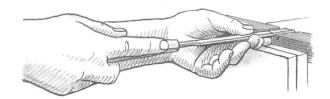

Chisel blades have two surfaces; one is flat and the other is beveled. Use the flat side to make deep cuts fairly quickly; be careful not to take out too much with it. The beveled side takes out less wood at a time, so it is slower. However, it's also the more cautious approach, so it's the best choice if you are not practiced with a chisel. To pare off excess wood with a chisel, hold the tool near the handle for control and push with the other hand. Make very light cuts.

2 Use a sliding bevel to transfer the angle to the wood and also to check the angle of the miter saw or machine fence.

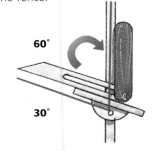

3 Miter blocks have slots cut into them, usually at 45 degrees and 90 degrees. When you insert a back saw into one of these slots, it guides the cut. Even though most miter boxes come with slots for just two angles, you can cut your own guides into wooden miter boxes for other angles. If you are using a metal, rather than a wooden miter box, you can minimize tearing on the bottom face by clamping a scrap piece of wood to the bottom of it.

4 The beauty of a mitered joint is that the grain continues around the joint to harmonize the design.

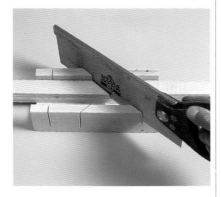

GLUING MITERED JOINTS

When you glue a mitered joint, make it easy by using 45 degree clamps. You can find these clamps at any hardware store. Alternatively, if you have enough C-clamps, you can temporarily glue "ears" to the mitered pieces and use clamps to pull them together.

USING GLUE

Make sure the glue is spread evenly and that you're using the correct amount. Ideally, you should see tiny droplets oozing out of the joint. If you don't see any glue, you might not have applied enough. If you put on too much, the joint will take a long time to dry. Use a damp cloth to wipe off excess glue.

FINISHING EDGES

Finishing work is very important with mitered joints. If the end grain is at all visible once the joint is formed, sand the ends of the slats until the surface is smooth and hard. You can chamfer the ends of the slats, but if you do so, make the chamfer consistent on all the slats. The block plane is ideal for this sort of work because the blade is located at a very low angle. This helps you trim awkward boards or end grain. You can also use a smoothing plane for this operation.

1 End grain is smoothed with a sanding block or—with great care—a block plane.

2 To chamfer a piece, mark it first and hold it down with clamps. Then start planing back with a smoothing plane. It's best to sand the ends first, across the grain, and then plane the long grain of the board.

3 Remove the arris, or sharp corner edges of the boards, by smoothing the edges with fine sandpaper.

PRE-FINISHING

Experienced woodworkers often apply the finish before they assemble the joint. This trick gives them faster, better results. It saves the time it would take to get a brush or cloth into inaccessible places and also prevents the glue from staining the wood during assembly. Do remember, though, not to finish the wood where it will be glued.

Safety

All woodworking tools are potentially dangerous, even a retracting steel tape, which can easily cut your finger. Whether blunt or sharp, any tool can hurt you if you use it inappropriately, although the general belief is that you are less likely to cut yourself with sharp tools than dull ones.

USING POWER TOOLS

Common sense reduces your risks of injuries, of course, but you need to take extra precautions when you use power tools. Always wear eye goggles; a headset or ear plugs, as appropriate; and a face mask over your nose and mouth. Gloves are helpful, but their bulkiness can get in the way and they can make your hands less sensitive. You can't feel the tool and sense how it is going—this can be dangerous.

HOLDING WOOD

Whether you are working with power or hand tools, it is essential that the wood you are cutting, planing or shaping is held securely in a vise or on a workbench. If the wood slips you may cut yourself. Beware also that splinters are a feature of many softwoods, especially those treated for outdoor use.

SANDING AND FINISHING

Always wear a dust mask when sanding by hand or with a power sander. Most finishes are safe to use, but make sure you follow the instructions and have a ready supply of solvent in case of spillages.

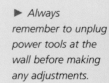

eye goggles

dust mask

ear protectors

▶ A table saw is a fearsome instrument: always keep your hands well away from the blade and use push sticks when ripping.

▼ A full-face mask gives total protection against flying particles and airborne dust.

▶ Always remember to unplug power tools at the wall before making any adjustments.

GENERAL SAFETY GUIDELINES

Make sure to pay attention to the following guidelines:
- Never put your fingers in front of a blade.
- Never wear loose-fitting clothing when you are working with tools.
- Never use too much force.
- If you feel nervous about a procedure, you are more likely to have an accident. Overconfidence is also risky.

Lumber

The projects in this book use dimensional lumber and sheets of plywood. Dimensional lumber comes in standard sizes. But the words that describe them can be confusing at first. For example, you might think that a 2 x 4 board is 2 inches thick and 4 inches wide, but it isn't. Instead, it's 1½ inches thick and 3½ inches wide. A 1 x 6 board measures ¾ inch thick by 5½ inches wide. If you want a piece of wood that is a full 1 inch thick by 5½ inches wide, ask for a 5/4 x 6 board, not a 1 x 6.

BUYING SOFTWOOD

At any home store or lumberyard, you'll find racks of softwood. It comes in various sizes. You can usually buy boards by the foot or meter and when this isn't possible, they will often cut it to length for you. Take your list of materials when you shop and make sure to buy more than enough in case you need it later.

▼ *Stacks of lumber in a large commercial kiln. The operator is collecting a sample from the middle of the pile to check for moisture content.*

DIMENSIONAL LUMBER SIZES

Nominal Size (inches)	Dressed Size (inches)	Dressed Size (millimeters)
1 x 1	¾ x ¾	19 x 19
1 x 2	¾ x 1½	19 x 38
1 x 3	¾ x 2½	19 x 64
1 x 4	¾ x 3½	19 x 89
1 x 6	¾ x 5½	19 x 140
1 x 8	¾ x 7¼	19 x 184
2 x 2	1½ x 1½	38 x 38
2 x 4	1½ x 3½	38 x 89
2 x 6	1½ x 5½	38 x 140
2 x 8	1½ x 7¼	38 x 184
4 x 4	3½ x 3½	89 x 89

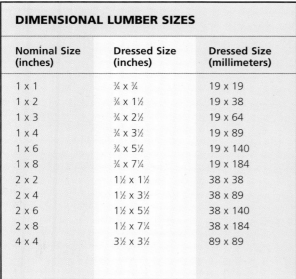

CHECKING FOR DEFECTS

When buying softwood it's worth sorting through the racks to find the best boards. Softwood isn't always stored well and as a result the boards are sometimes defective. Watch for the following defects.

1. Decay

Don't buy lumber that looks as if it has been sitting in moisture.

2. Insect attack

Don't buy wood with small holes or tunnels. The insect that caused them may be gone, but the wood will be weakened by the damage. If you notice it only after you've gotten it home, don't put it in a scrap pile in case the insect is still there.

3. Checking

If wood has seasoned too quickly, the ends can check, or crack, because of shrinkage. These boards may be fine in the middle, but it's best not to buy them because you'll have to waste the ends and the board could have other problems. Never buy a board with a crack right through it, either.

4. Splits

The ends of a piece of wood may split as it seasons because the ends dry more quickly than the middle. Buy these pieces only if you are going to cut off the ends anyway, but don't pay for the split ends.

5. Loose knots

Try to avoid knotty wood because knots show through most finishes and invariably land just where you'll need to cut a joint. Number 1 grade soft-wood and number 1 clear pine, for example, do not have knots. Any grade from number 2 down is likely to have some. Choose your grade according to the way you'll use the wood, but never buy a piece with loose knots.

WOOD ON THE MOVE

The projects use softwood in narrow sizes that are unlikely to be cupped. Long boards are often bowed along their length. Don't buy extremely bowed wood. Although you may end up cutting the boards to shorter lengths, so the curve won't be so pronounced, it's still best to choose straight lengths of wood.

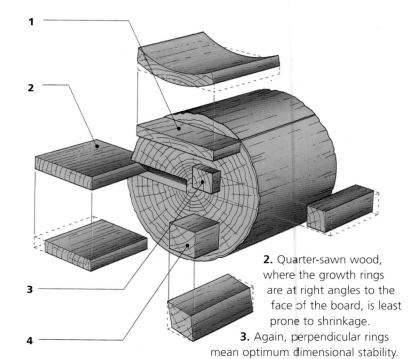

1. Wide boards will shrink more in width than in length or thickness, and cup away from the tree's heart.

2. Quarter-sawn wood, where the growth rings are at right angles to the face of the board, is least prone to shrinkage.

3. Again, perpendicular rings mean optimum dimensional stability.

4. Square sections with diagonally-running growth rings will tend to distort to a rhombus.

BUYING SHEET MATERIALS

Sheet materials are a joy to buy and use because they don't cup, twist, or check. They may be heavy and awkward when bought, but they simplify most woodworking operations. They are usually available in 4 x 8 foot (1200 x 2400mm) sheets of various thicknesses. A lumberyard or home store may offer to make a few free cuts so it will be easier to get the sheets home. For a little extra money, they will make all your cuts.

Plywood

We have chosen plywood for some of the projects because it is available everywhere, and often in smaller sizes than full sheets. It comes in various thicknesses and grades. For garden furniture, we recommend marine or exterior-grade plywood. Birch ply is the best quality, and the most expensive.

GLUING WOOD

Water-resistant wood glue is the best choice for these projects. Both yellow and white glues are popular. No matter what kind of glue you use, you apply it the same way. Make sure your glue bottle isn't full of old bits of dried adhesive. These will affect the joint.

Joints

1 Apply a bead of glue to both sides of the joint. Use your finger or a thin piece of wood to spread the glue across the joint. Too much glue and the joint will be difficult to position; too little and the joint will be weak.

2 Screw the pieces into position while the glue is still wet. This pulls the gluing faces together and makes for a much stronger joint.

Wooden plugs

1 Hardwood plugs are used to hide unsightly screwheads. Squeeze a drop or two of glue into a hole counterbored to the plug's diameter.

2 Locate the plug and drive home with a mallet. Remove protruding material with a chisel or finish saw and sand smooth with a block.

ALTERNATIVE LUMBER OPTIONS

Commercially available softwood—usually pine or spruce—is the easiest type of lumber to cut and work, and is ideal for those with limited skills and few tools. For strength and longevity, however, hardwoods are the optimum choice, although they cost substantially more, and require a greater level of skill to work successfully.

Cedar

Instead of a hardwood you might choose cedar. It is one of the most durable softwoods and is very popular for decking and garden furniture.

Douglas fir

Douglas fir is commonly used for outdoor structures, particularly for arbors and pergolas. It is strong and durable, so it's ideal for garden furniture.

Oak

Oak is a popular choice for its texture and grain, although its honey coloring will turn gray unless you protect it or store it inside. It can be difficult to work because it is so hard, but it will give many years of pleasure. You can find white oak or red oak, both of which are good for outdoor furniture.

Teak

Teak has been used to make boats as well as garden furniture for centuries. It is strong and durable and has an oily texture that stands up to moisture well. Its color varies from pale yellow-brown in the sapwood to dark brown in the heartwood.

Finishes

Outdoor furniture and accessories have to stand up to wind, rain and sunlight. Fortunately, you can apply various finishes and preservatives to prolong the life of wood in the yard. Lumberyards and garden centers also sell pretreated wood that can be used for outdoor projects.

PAINTING

You don't have to leave wood with a plain finish. Paint is a colorful way to protect it, but to make it last, you have to learn how to prepare the wood as well as apply it.

1 Apply white shellac to knots. The shellac forms a barrier between the knot and the primer and prevents resin from seeping through the paint. This is particularly important for softwoods, which tend to be more resinous than hardwoods.

2 Fill any cracks in the wood with wood filler, let the filler dry and sand smooth and level. Take particular care when you fill countersunk screw heads because they take quite a bit of filler that may dip when it dries. Add a little more filler if it does.

3 Sand in three steps. First, use coarse sandpaper, then a medium grade and end with fine sandpaper.

4 Apply wood primer with a 2 inch (50mm) paintbrush. Make sure to work the primer into all the hard-to-reach places. Wood primer helps to bond the paint to the wood. Allow the primer to dry thoroughly.

5 Working with the grain, apply the first coat of paint. Paint hard-to-reach places first and smooth out any rough spots between these areas and the body of the piece.

6 Once the first coat is dry, go over it with a tack cloth to remove any dust. Apply the second coat of paint and allow it to dry overnight.

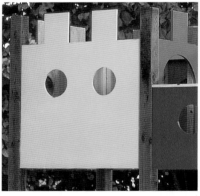

7 Two coats are often enough, but depending on the shade of paint you might want to add a third. Paint very carefully for a great result that will last. These days many exterior paints are latex- (water) based, making them easier to use and faster drying than oil-based products.

FILLING HOLES

In many of these projects you need to fill sunken nailheads, countersunk screw heads and gaps in joints. If you intend to paint the object, the color of the filler doesn't matter very much. But if you are using a clear or even an opaque finish, choose your filler carefully. It's best to use a filler that is a little darker than the wood you are filling because it looks more like a natural fault.

1 Apply the filler with a flexible putty knife. Spread the filler over the fault, building up the surface until it is smooth but slightly raised. Once the filler is dry and flaky, you can sand it.

2 If you can't find the right filler color, you can mix sawdust from the original wood with white or yellow wood glue. Add the sawdust until it is thick and workable and mix it thoroughly. It takes longer to dry than most commercially available fillers so you'll need to leave it longer—usually at least two hours. When thoroughly dry, sand it smooth.

STAINING WOOD

Many people want to make their projects look aged, so they stain the wood. You have two options for coloring wood without hiding the grain. You can use varnishes that are already mixed with stain or you can stain the wood first and then protect and enhance it with the clear finish of your choice. The latter technique gives you more flexibility and also allows the stain to soak more deeply into the wood. Colored varnishes can look as if they are sitting on the surface, but they give a more even result when a wood resists a stain.

1 Test your chosen finish on a scrap of wood before using it on the whole project. You can darken a stain by applying varnish or oil to the wood after you've stained it. You can also make a stain darker by adding more coats, but remember, you can't ever make it lighter.

2 Fill and sand the project, remembering that finishes amplify any defects in the bare wood.

3 Apply the stain. Make sure always to have enough stain on your brush. If you let a stained edge dry—and this can happen quickly—you risk leaving a mark.

4 Let the stain dry but don't sand it. Then apply two coats of clear varnish or polyurethane, sanding with fine sandpaper between the coats once the first one is dry. It's important to sand between coats because varnish and polyurethane raise the grain on wood. You also sand between coats of precolored varnishes.

SAVING WOOD FROM ROT

Paint is certainly one option for protecting wood from rot and decay, but there are others. You can choose to make the projects from a more durable lumber than softwood, but that increases the cost. Less expensive but more durable woods include cedar, cypress, Douglas fir and redwood.

OILING YOUR PROJECT

Oil products, usually containing linseed oil, are increasingly popular because the oils are natural. Oils keep the wood moist. You need to reapply them once a year, but they are very easy to apply and an oil finish doesn't peel or flake.

1 Fill any knotholes, gaps and sunken nails or screws with wood filler and sand after the filler dries. Apply the first coat of oil with a brush or cloth, rubbing it in with a nylon scouring pad.

2 After ten minutes or so, use a clean cloth to wipe off the excess oil. Otherwise, it can harden as a gooey mess. Once the oil is dry—this usually takes about 48 hours—apply a second coat. Between the coats, rub the wood with a nylon scouring pad. Keep applying coats until you've created a good finish.

PROTECTING WOOD IN THE GARDEN				
Type of Finish	Ease of Application	Protection	Cost	Maintenance
Polyurethane	Medium	Medium	Medium	Renew every couple of years
Wood treatment	Easy	Good	Medium	Low
Oil	Easy	Low to medium	Medium	High
Paint	Medium to hard	Good	Medium	Low to medium

INSPIRATION AND PROJECTS

Here you'll find a number of very stylish and elegant projects that can be made by following the straightforward step-by-step instructions. In "Pots and Planters" you'll learn how to make a classic planter, a planter bench and a raised planter that can double as a water feature, while the largest section—"Sitting and Eating"—covers a variety of stylish chairs, benches and tables. "Divisions and Doorways" includes trellis screens and arches to make private spaces or show off particular aspects of your garden, plus we show you how to attract birds and butterflies in "Wildlife Winners." Finally, the "Leisure" section gives a diverse range of projects for the whole family to enjoy.

As well as displaying 20 projects that you can make, this section introduces you to commercially available products and covers all the major types of garden furniture and features.

PURPOSEFUL PLANTING

ATTRACTING BUTTERFLIES

Butterflies feed on plants that grow in the sun, so be sure to pick a bright spot for this planter. Container plants that attract butterflies include:

Agastache
Aster
Cleome
Coreopsis
Cosmos
Nicotiana
Rudbeckia
Salvia

WINTER COLOR

Try mixing evergreens with hardier flowering plants to bring some height variations to a winter planter. The following plants and trees will survive all but the most severe temperatures:

Bulbs (such as dwarf narcissus)
Dwarf conifers
Heathers
Ornamental cabbages
Primulas
Spruce
Trailing ivy
Variegated grasses
Violas

Ivy

BUG DETERRENTS

If you live near water or feel plagued by insects during the summer months, consider adding some of these plants to your containers. Lay a mulch of cedarwood chippings for extra effect.

Citronella
False nettle
Lemonbalm
Licorice
Pennyroyal
Peppermint
Southernwood

◀ *Use decorative containers of herbs and flowers to bring fragrance and color to even the darkest corner of your garden.*

Planters and Pots

Container gardening is a great way to make full use of limited outdoor space. While pots and planters can be placed to spectacular effect in large gardens, marking entrances or enlivening dull corners, they really come into their own when grouped in a confined space. Planters present a wonderful opportunity to feature even your tropical indoor plants outdoors for the summer season. Apartment balconies, backyards and intimate courtyard settings can all be transformed by the judicious use of carefully selected and planted containers.

A PANOPLY OF CHOICE

The range of containers is vast, from imposing antique lead urns to small brightly colored plastic pots, with every variation in between. They can be bought in just about any shape or size, in natural or manufactured materials, with pretty ornamentation or modishly plain, and in every imaginable color.

Alternatively you can build your own planter, in which case your only constraints will be the size of your garden, the reach of your budget and the extent of your woodworking skills. With only a minimum of each, as this chapter shows, you can build a feature that will grace your garden or balcony for years to come.

CHOOSING YOUR PLANTER

Almost any container with holes in the base can be used as a planter. While wooden planters and ceramic pots are traditional favorites, old metal buckets, birdcages and car tires can all be used to great effect. Even if your space is very limited—on a balcony, for example—you can still find a satisfying form of self-expression through your choice of planter and planting.

Whether you build, improvise or buy, it is important to consider the requirements and attributes of your garden as well as those of any potential planter.

- Are you looking to introduce instant height into an area of your garden? If so, consider the relative merits of three-tiered planters, tall pots, wall-mounted containers or ground planters with climber structures. Each one will form a different shape and require a different kind of planting.
- How large a space do you want to plant? Would one large container be adequate? Or would you prefer several smaller ones? One large planter will dry out more slowly and can hold bigger plants, but you may achieve more variety with a group of smaller pots in complementary designs, perhaps at differing heights.
- How important is ease of maintenance? If you are often away from home or if water access is limited, larger containers in non-drying materials are probably the answer. Most containers require watering at least once a day in summer, and feeding once a week.
- Would you prefer to install a very mobile form of garden, where you can shift the "furniture" around? Or do you want to make a permanent statement, with stability a key issue?
- What kind of weather does your garden enjoy? Most container plants require at least five hours of sunshine each day. If your site is very windy or bathed in very hot sunlight all day, you may need to build some form of screening to protect delicate plants. If you live in a cold climate, you may need to choose more mobile planters to bring pots indoors during the winter. On the other hand, if you live in a hot climate, consider using lighter-colored containers to lessen heat absorption.

Materials

The kind of material you favor for your planters will be influenced by your site and budget as much as your preferred style. Choose a long-lasting, frost-proof material wherever possible. Another point to bear in mind is the weight of the container. In most cases you will need to put the planter in position before filling it with soil mix and plants, as they will significantly increase the overall weight. This is especially important if you are using planters on a balcony or other weight-sensitive areas.

◀ ▲ *These pine planters (left) have been treated using non-toxic preservative but still retain their natural color. The classic shapes of shrubs, such as pineapple guava, complement the formality of the setting (above), while the overflowing ivy and explosion of chrysanthemums soften the edges of the planters.*

WOOD
Wooden planters come in a multitude of shapes and sizes, from elegant square planters with finials to rustic half-barrel containers. When buying or self-building, choose a hardwood such as redwood or cedar to reduce the risk of rot, and paint the inside of any wooden container with non-toxic, water-based preservative.

The outside of a wooden planter, of course, can be painted in any color

you choose, and there are now many different colors of preservative available to decorate and preserve the wood simultaneously.

STONE
Stone containers can be plain or sculptural, with prices to match. It is worth considering all the options here very carefully before buying, as the planters should last for life. If you are irresistibly drawn to a very fine

▶ *The rustic simplicity of the barrel is echoed by the charm of chrysanthemums, which tone perfectly with the shade of the wood.*

ornate urn with decorative top edging, be careful not to obscure this costly feature by covering the edge with trailing plants.

CLAY AND TERRA COTTA

These pots are perhaps the most commonly used form of planter. They may be plain, ornamented, painted or glazed. Terra cotta dries out rapidly, and any plants will need frequent watering, unless they are double potted (where a smaller pot sits inside a larger one, with the space between filled by sphagnum or peat moss). Glazed ceramic pots are less prone to drying out and less likely to suffer frost damage, but check for drainage holes, as they are often sold without them.

▲ ▶ Terra cotta planters (above right) come in a huge range of shapes and sizes. Unglazed terra cotta ages beautifully as salts and minerals leach through the clay. The painted wooden planter (right) lends itself to a classic white and red arrangement.

▲ ▶ Restricting the use of material to terra cotta (above) helps to emphasize the dramatic shapes of the containers while preventing them from overwhelming the planting. Stone (at right) is the classic material for planter construction. It works well with almost any planting theme, blends into its surroundings and is virtually indestructible.

LEAD AND METAL

Traditional garden containers made of lead are fairly costly, but they can look stunning in a formal garden or when used to add a subtle focus to a small area. Try to place them immediately into their final position, as they will be virtually impossible to move when filled with plants.

This form of container is certainly among the most durable, but many gardeners are concerned about the possibility of lead runoff into the soil. Fortunately some superb faux-lead planters are available that avoid this problem; they also have the added advantage of being lightweight.

Other types of metal containers include steel, which can add a bright, contemporary look to the garden. Wirework and wrought-iron planters come in many different designs, from simple basket shapes to explosions of curlicues and flourishes. Part of their appeal lies in revealing the rich, brown soil that is usually hidden from view, or a lining of moss growing between the wires.

▲ *Galvanized steel, polished steel and wirework containers are available in a wide range of styles to suit all tastes. They are ideal for bringing a modern decorative touch to the garden and are relatively inexpensive to buy.*

▲ *Lead planters are among the most coveted types of container. Here, a lead planter provides the perfect foil for the formal spiral topiary of a holly bush.*

◄ ► *This two-tiered wrought-iron planter (left) would provide the perfect setting for a cascading display of blooms. The weight and color of this lead chest (right) are lightened by a profusion of azaleas.*

◄ The explosion of plants in this wirework stand (left) is ideal for a country cottage garden. The combination of direct planting and terra cotta pots increases the sense of fecundity.

▼ Plastic planters come in a huge variety of shapes, sizes and colors. You will always find one to suit your garden. They are lightweight, which can be an advantage, but you may need to assess carefully what you plant in them and where you put them.

CONCRETE

Concrete is increasingly used in bold, geometric shapes in contemporary gardens. It can be colored to suit any garden scheme or "aged" by applying a coat of milk or yogurt. The bacteria in the milk or yoghurt will promote the growth of moss and algae, which rapidly ages the look of the concrete.

PLASTIC

Plastic is the least expensive, lowest-maintenance material you can use for planters. Unfortunately, its man-made quality can also look unnatural in a garden, unless virtually covered by trailing plants or heavily disguised to look like lead or terra cotta. If you want a very modern, deliberately "unnatural" look, however, plastic could be just the thing.

Plastic retains moisture far longer than clay or terra cotta but deteriorates fast in sunlight, making it ideal for use as the inner part of a double planter. These can be preplanted and the plants brought to glorious maturity elsewhere, before being moved into position in a window box, for example.

IMPROVISED CONTAINERS

If you are looking for a chance to express some real individualism, almost anything can be used as a plant container, as long as it is possible to insert drainage holes in the base. Stone sinks have long been a favorite. Clay drainage pipes can be used to add height and quirkiness to a garden, just as chimney pots are used in Europe, where they are available as reproductions or "antiques."

All sorts of wooden objects will double up quite happily as planters. Wooden wheelbarrows, which have the added bonus of being highly transportable, make ideal large containers. Flower boxes, wine crates and wooden or metal birdcages can all act as the starting point for some inspired container planting. If you want to introduce more metal into the garden, pitchers, milk jugs, watering cans and even old filing cabinets are fun to play with—just let your imagination loose!

◄ A traditional wooden planter on the rail of a balcony can be filled with plants such as ivy, pansies and prairie mallows to create a garden in the tiniest of spaces. The planter here has been screwed to the rail for safety.

◄ With a bit of imagination, any receptacle can be turned into an attractive and unique planter. Here, the rustic charm of an old wheelbarrow is softened and enhanced by a variety of trailing plants and large gourds.

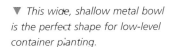

▼ This wide, shallow metal bowl is the perfect shape for low-level container planting.

◄ Hanging baskets and window boxes give a garden greater height and visual interest. The hanging baskets (far left) are lined with sphagnum moss and filled with trailing plants, while the shape of the window box (near left) is echoed by the staggered heights of the pelargoniums.

COMPARISON OF CONTAINER TYPES AND MATERIALS

Characteristics	Wood	Stone	Terra cotta	Lead	Concrete	Plastic/Glass Fiber
Durability	Good if treated; check for splintering or warping	Exceptionally good	Needs careful handling; may crack with impact	Extremely durable: can be expected to last hundreds of years	Exceptionally good	Glass fiber is very durable; plastic may deteriorate fast under extremes of temperature
Weight	Medium weight	Extremely heavy	Fairly heavy	The heaviest form of container	Very heavy	Extremely light
Frost-proofing	Good when treated; may crack with sudden change of temperature	Exceptionally good	Unglazed pots will crack with frost; heavy glazing lends protection	Totally frost-proof	Totally frost-proof	Plastic pots can crack under frost
Water Retention	Depends on planter style; may benefit from use of an inner container	Good; check to see drainage holes exist	Unglazed pots soak up water and require frequent watering; glazed pots retain water	Total water retention; ensure drainage holes exist or use inner container	Total water retention; ensure drainage holes exist or use inner container	Total water retention; useful as inner containers
Cost	Medium	Medium to high	Low to medium	High to exceptionally high	Low to medium	Low

Classic Planter

Planters suit a wide range of locations in a patio or yard. They brighten up shady corners, and a matching pair look stylish when used to mark an entrance or the beginning of a path. This one is in classic style, with moldings applied to the side panels and finials at the corners.

It is also on the large side; a shrub or even a small tree could be potted in it or planted in a pot set in the planter. You could make a smaller version by reducing the dimensions all round.

Line the inside of the planter with polyethylene if you are filling it with a soil mix, and treat the whole piece with wood preservative. Pay particular attention to the bottoms of the legs, as they will be subject to attack by moisture. Paint the planter in any color you like or apply wood stain and/or clear or colored varnish.

▶ With its formal shape and classic panel molding, this planter makes the perfect container for the tapering elegance of a small conifer, such as the miniature juniper shown here.

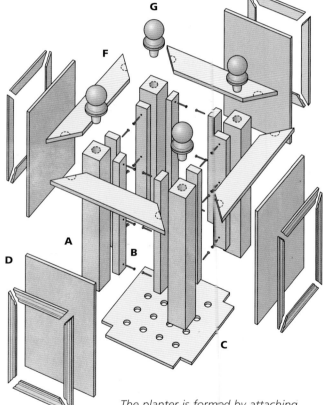

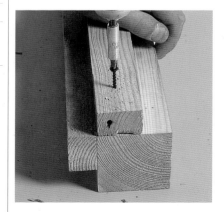

1 Make sure the ends of the legs (A) are square. Drill and countersink the leg battens (B) and glue and screw two battens to adjacent faces of each leg, flush with the sides and the top of the legs, but 2½ inches (65mm) from the bottom to accommodate the planter base.

The planter is formed by attaching battens to the four legs, and then attaching the side panels and base to these battens. Mitered molding and finials provide the classic decoration.

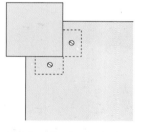

Fig. 2.1

depth of notch d = 2½ in. (65mm)

2 Cut the plywood base (C) and sides (D) to size using a handsaw, which causes less splintering than a jigsaw and is easier to keep straight. Then cut notches in the corners of the base so that it fits around the bottoms of the legs (fig. 2.1).

3 Drill and countersink the base around the notches and screw to the bottom of the battens on two of the legs. Use screws that go at least 1 inch (25mm) into the battens, but screw them in carefully or you may split the wood.

4 Once you've screwed the base between a pair of legs, fit two of the sides, gluing and nailing them to the leg battens and the base.

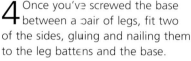

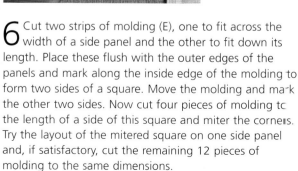

5 With two of the side panels in place, attach the remaining two legs and side panels. Finally, use a nail set to knock the nailheads below the surface for filling.

6 Cut two strips of molding (E), one to fit across the width of a side panel and the other to fit down its length. Place these flush with the outer edges of the panels and mark along the inside edge of the molding to form two sides of a square. Move the molding and mark the other two sides. Now cut four pieces of molding to the length of a side of this square and miter the corners. Try the layout of the mitered square on one side panel and, if satisfactory, cut the remaining 12 pieces of molding to the same dimensions.

TONGUE AND GROOVE SIDES

For a more rustic appearance, screw lengths of tongue and groove softwood to the plywood sides in place of the molding. Attach each length of tongue and groove with three screws, at the top, middle and bottom, all lined up along the center of each board (fig. A). Don't butt the boards tightly together; instead, give each one an expansion gap inside the groove of about ⅛ inch (3mm). To create enough space for the tongue and groove, reposition the plywood side panels by using 1 x 1 in. battens on the legs (fig. B).

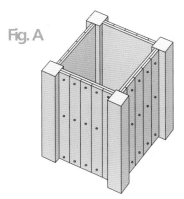

Fig. A

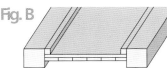

Fig. B

Alternatively, you can use the framed construction we've chosen for the Double Planter Bench (page 42) and apply the tongue and groove to the framework (fig. C). Line the inside with plywood before planting.

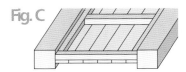

Fig. C

7 Clamp one piece of molding in position along the marked line for reference, then glue and nail the other three lengths in place. Remove the clamp and glue and nail the fourth piece. Tap all of the nailheads below the surface with a nail set. Repeat on the remaining three sides.

9 Drill holes for the finials using a spade bit. Finials vary in size from one make to another, so make sure you use a spade bit of a size that gives you a snug, but not tight, fit for the finial. Glue the finials into the holes, making sure that any tear-out around the holes is hidden. Use the spade bit to drill about 20 holes in the base of the planter for drainage. Try to stop drilling with the spade bit when the point pierces through to the other side of the plywood, then drill from the other side to reduce tear-out.

8 Cut the miters on the fascia pieces (F) and do a dry-run assembly to check for fit. Once you're satisfied, glue and nail the fascia pieces to the tops of the legs. Find the center points along each joint to locate the finials (G).

10 Fill all the nail and screw holes with wood filler and sand smooth. Filler typically contracts in countersunk screw holes, so leave it overnight after sanding in case the filler dips and you need to add more. Then apply wood preservative and your choice of paint, stain, and/or varnish. If you want to add a waterproof lining to the planter, see the instructions given for the Double Planter Bench on page 45.

Double Planter Bench

Take a pair of planters, join them together with joists and slats, and you have a planter bench that combines two of the most useful items in any yard or garden. The style is contemporary, with the vertical slats of the planters complementing the horizontal ones on the seat, and would suit a city balcony or patio where space is at a premium.

You can make countless modifications to the design—add a back, for example, or even use posts and a trellis to make sides and a roof for climbers. The planter-bench combination offers a compact solution that you can easily size up or down for two or more people or to suit larger or smaller plants.

▶ *This planter bench comfortably seats two people but can easily be adapted by increasing the length of the seat rails and joists.*

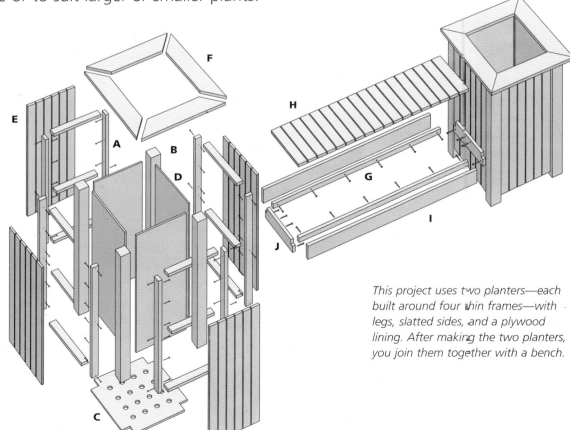

This project uses two planters—each built around four thin frames—with legs, slatted sides, and a plywood lining. After making the two planters, you join them together with a bench.

1 Make up four frames (A) for the first planter. Anchor the frames against a stop as shown below while you glue and nail the components together. Use two nails for each joint.

2 Make sure the ends of the legs (B) are square. Align all four legs against a straightedge and mark a line 2½ inches (65mm) from one end. This indicates the location of the lower edge of the frame. It is important to align the legs accurately because the slightest variation will keep the planter from sitting flat.

3 On the same face, mark a line approximately 1 inch (24mm) from the edge of each leg as a position guide for the frames. This measurement doesn't have to be exact as long as it is consistent from leg to leg.

4 Glue and nail the long side of one frame to one of the legs, aligning it with the vertical and horizontal marks. The top of the frame should be flush with the top of the leg.

Fig. 5.1

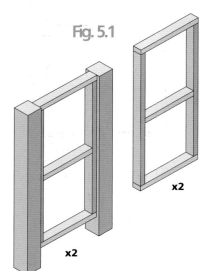

x2

x2

5 Glue and nail the opposite side of the frame to a second leg in exactly the same way. Repeat these steps to join the other two legs with one frame. You now have two sets of legs and frame and two extra frames (fig. 5.1).

6 Lay one frame and leg assembly on the ground. Mark a pencil line on each leg as before to position the frames, then glue and nail a frame to each leg. The construction is now beginning to take shape, although it will wobble a bit at this stage.

NAILING THE FRAMES

When assemblinc the frames, it's best to use two rails for each joint. If you angle the nails a little, it creates a dovetail effect and helps to pull the joint together. To improve access when nailing against a stop, raise the frame with a piece of scrap wood.

7 Lay the other frame-and-leg assembly on the ground and flip the three-frame assembly so that it sits on top. (It's useful to have an assistant to help here.) Align the frames on the legs on the ground and glue and nail them in place.

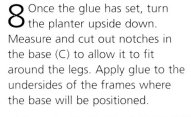

8 Once the glue has set, turn the planter upside down. Measure and cut out notches in the base (C) to allow it to fit around the legs. Apply glue to the undersides of the frames where the base will be positioned.

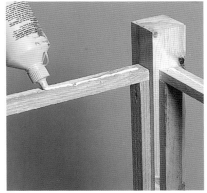

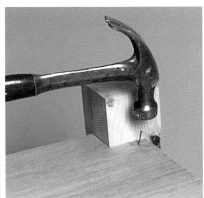

9 Position the plywood base and nail it to the bottom of the frame. You can use screws if you prefer, but all that drilling and countersinking adds significantly to the time it takes for relatively little added strength.

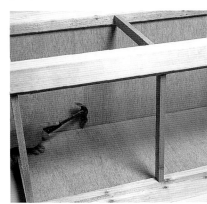

10 Now cut four pieces of plywood measuring 24 x 38 inches (600 x 950mm): this is the lining for the sides of the planter (D). Lay the lining pieces inside the frames and nail them in position (fig. 10.1). Note that the lining is nailed to the frame components, not to the legs.

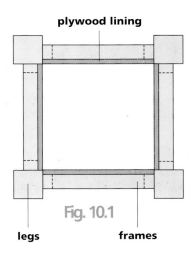

plywood lining

Fig. 10.1

legs   **frames**

MARKING THE SEAT JOISTS

Many woodworking projects contain repetitive operations. If you can think of a way to carry out several of these together, you'll save time and often improve accuracy, too. Mark both seat joists for drilling at the same time, using a piece of wood cut to the width of the required distance between the drill centers as your marking gauge.

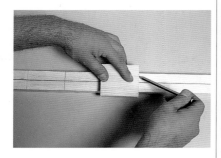

CONCEALED FIXING OF THE PLANTER SLATS

If you want to avoid having to fill nail holes on the planter slats, you could screw the slats in place from inside the planter. You'd have to do that before attaching the plywood lining, however, when the assembly is still very unstable, and it would require some awkward drilling.

11 You can now add the slatted sides. Examine the slats (E) and sand any rough edges. Nail the slats to the frames, using spacers to position them, and sink the heads with a nail set. We used ⅜ inch (10mm) spacers, but you may need to adjust this. To adjust, lay the slats—one against the next—up against one of the legs. Measure the gap between the last slat and the other leg, and divide by the number of spaces required (one more than the number of slats). The answer equals the thickness of the spacer required.

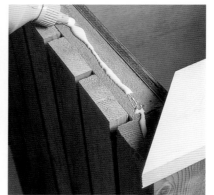

12 The fascia hides and protects the end grain on the slats. Lay the fascia pieces (F) on the planter top, aligning the inside edge with the inside of the planter, and mark the position of the miter cut on the inside and outside of each corner. Miter the fascia pieces (see pages 20–21) and glue and nail to the framework, sinking the heads with a nail set. The first planter is now finished; construct the second in exactly the same manner.

13 Mark a centerline on one face of the seat joists (G). Calculate the required spacing of the seat slats (H) as you did for the side slats in Step 11. Drill and countersink holes in the joists along the centerline at the required intervals so that the seat slats are spaced evenly along them (see sidebar).

14 The slats are attached to the joists from below so there are no screw or nail heads to collect water. Using spacers to keep the slats the required distance apart, screw the joists to the slats, ensuring that they remain flush with the slat ends. Any slight irregularities can be sanded smooth later.

MORE SUPPORT FOR THE BASE

A large volume of soil becomes very heavy when wet, so add a central block for extra support if you are filling the planter with soil mix, and remember to drill drainage holes in the planter bases.

LINING THE PLANTERS

Planters filled with soil mix will have an extended lifespan if you protect the plywood lining by painting it with polyurethane varnish or by lining the sides and base with polyethylene sheeting. Don't forget to punch drainage holes through the bottom of the sheeting to let water out.

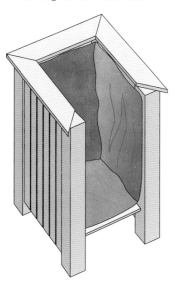

15 Align the seat rails (I), which act as a front and back to the bench, so that their tops and ends are flush with the seat slats. Clamp and screw the seat joists to the rails. The bench should now be pretty sturdy.

16 Make the seat supports (J) by gluing together offcuts from the plywood lining sheets. Cut notches in the two top corners to accept the joists on the underside of the seat slats. Mark the planters at the desired height for the bench—18 inches (450mm) is a good starting point, but adjust this to suit your preference. Drill and countersink the supports, then glue and screw them to the planters.

17 The bench seat fits neatly onto the support as the seat joists locate in the notches. Attach the seat to the planters by screwing through the front and back rails into the plywood supports.

18 It is best to detach the planters from the bench before you apply preservative, paint, stain, and/or varnish. Don't forget to clean up any dried adhesive spills and sand them back; otherwise, you'll be left with a bare patch where the stain doesn't take.

Raised Planter with Water Feature

YOU WILL NEED

Inner side panels (A)
Four 26 in. (660mm) 1 x 8 softwood

Corner posts (B)
Four 9 in. (230mm) 4 x 4 fence post

Outer side panels (C)
One 14 ft. (4270mm) 1 x 8 softwood

Caps (D)
Four ¾ in. (19mm) 4 x 4 marine plywood

Finials (E)
Four decorative finials or fence post tops

Hardware and finishing

24 plastic corner joints

Small water feature kit with reservoir, pump and fountain head

One hundred 1 in. (25mm) #8 galvanized screws

Wood preservative, paint, stain, varnish

Tools

Basic tool kit plus spade bit large enough to make holes for finials

This versatile planter is quick and easy to construct. It makes an attractive addition to any patio or deck and would look equally striking in a sunroom, conservatory or other indoor setting.

As the planter will be in contact with water, all surfaces, and especially the end grain, must be treated with wood preservative. Alternatively, you can paint it a color of your choice and finish it with several coats of polyurethane varnish. If the planter is to be sited indoors, a waterproof base must be attached to contain the soil.

▶ *This freestanding water garden shows off an architectural design of pebbles and mauve-flowering hebe. The finished structure is full of life and sound.*

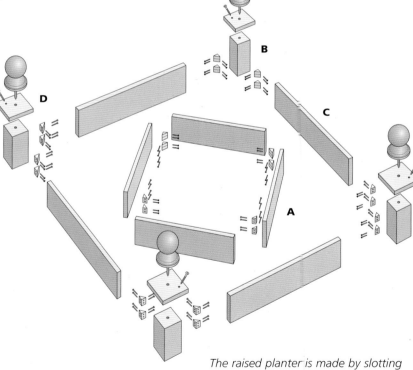

The raised planter is made by slotting one small box diagonally inside a larger box, with the water feature sitting proudly in the center of the smaller box.

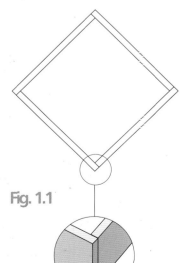

Fig. 1.1

1 First construct the inner box. Carefully cut the inner side panels (A) to size using a handsaw, ensuring that the ends are square. Using the corner joints, join two of the boards together in a butt joint as shown. Join the remaining boards in a similar fashion (see fig. 1.1) until the box is complete.

3 Cut the fence post to size using a handsaw to make the corner posts (B). Measure and mark the position of the corner joints, and screw four to each post.

4 Measure, mark and cut the sides of the outer box (C) using a handsaw. Screw the sides to the corner posts, ensuring that the bases sit squarely on the floor.

2 Measure diagonally across the outside edge of the box. This gives you the length of the four sides of the outer box. Reduce this figure by 2 inches (50mm) to allow for the corner posts (see fig. 2.1).

Fig. 2.1

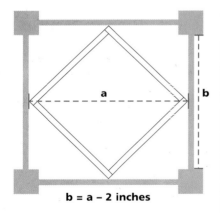

b = a − 2 inches

5 Find the center of each corner post by drawing diagonals across them. Drill a pilot hole for the finial screw where the diagonals intersect.

6 Drill holes for the finials in the center of the plywood offcut "caps" using a spade bit. Finials vary in size from one make to another, so make sure you use a spade bit of a size that gives you a snug, but not tight, fit for the finial. After aligning the two pieces via the pilot holes, attach the caps to the corner post tops with small screws driven in off-center and at an angle.

MAKING YOUR OWN WATER FEATURE

Line the smaller box with pond liner held in place with lengths of 1 x 1 treated softwood batten screwed to the inside edges approximately 2 inches (50 mm) down from the top. This becomes the reservoir.

Locate a low-voltage submersible pump centrally in the base of the reservoir. Drill a hole for the cable, thread it through and seal with silicone sealant.

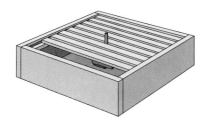

Board over the reservoir with lengths of 2 x 1 treated softwood batten, leaving 1 inch (25mm) gaps for the water to run back through. Position the pump outlet between two battens and affix the fountain head. Decorate with plants and pebbles.

7 Locate the finials (E) in the pilot holes and screw down firmly. Position the inner box inside the outer box and at diagonals to it.

9 You may find it cheaper to buy a ready-made water feature than to buy a pump on its own. Put the plastic reservoir, pump and cover into the center box, drill a hole for the cable and seal with silicone sealant.

8 You may wish to screw the boxes together, but strictly speaking it is not necessary, as the weight of their contents will keep the components from moving around.

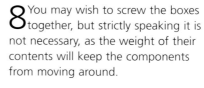

10 Fill the reservoir with water, cover with stones and turn on the pump. If you prefer the option of an overflowing pot, simply drill a hole the same size as the water pump outlet in the bottom of the pot, push the plastic outlet through the hole and seal in position with silicone sealant. Fill the outer box with soil and position plants to complete.

PURPOSEFUL PLANTING

SHADE

Awnings and umbrellas help to keep the sun off your outdoor dining area, but you can also choose climbing plants and trees that will provide good shade.

Cherry trees
   (*Prunus* spp.)
Eucalyptus trees
   (*Eucalyptus* spp.)
Indian bean (*Catalpa bignonioides*)
Paperbark maple
   (*Acer griseum*)
Tree hazel
   (*Corylus colurna*)
Various vines

Eucalyptus

Virginia creeper (*Parthenocissus quinquefolia*)
Weeping willow (*Salix babylonica*)
Wisteria (*Wisteria* spp.)

HERBS

Herbs make fantastic plants for any garden, balcony or patio as they are both goodlooking and useful. You don't need much to add zest to your favourite dishes

Common basil (*Ocinum basilicum*)

Fennel (*Foeniculum vulgare*)

Garlic (*Allium satium*)

Oregano (*Origanum heracleoticum*)

Salad chervil
   (*Anthriscus cerefolium*)

Spearmint
   (*Mentha spicata*)

Sweet balm
   (*Melissa officinalis*)

Common basil

◄ *Sets of folding furniture combine elegance with practicality. The subtle curves of this hardwood table and chairs are the perfect design choice for an idyllic waterlily pond location.*

Sitting and Eating

Eating and drinking under an overhanging vine with sunlight shimmering through the leaves is a tantalizing idea. You'll just need some chairs and a table, maybe something to keep the drinks cool, and a wheeled cart or tray to bring refreshments from the kitchen. Any balcony or patio can be transformed into a dining area. The breadth of design is so wide that you can complement contemporary or classic garden styles with outdoor furniture you can buy or make.

CHOOSING OUTDOOR FURNITURE

Outdoor furniture is available in all styles, materials, and prices. You can find tables that stay outdoors all year, and chairs that fold up for indoor storage. Lounge chairs offer a laid-back approach to outdoor life, while Lutyens benches (see photograph on page 60) add a classic formality to a garden. Consider the portability of outdoor furniture, its durability and maintenance, and shapes and sizes to suit your needs.

- Will your furniture be placed on a lawn or a paved area? Heavy hardwood furniture can be difficult to move when mowing; lightweight stacking chairs may be more suitable for sitting and eating on the grass. Remember that furniture may sink into a damp lawn if the legs taper to fine points.

▲ *Intricate wrought-iron styles of furniture add a classical air to any garden and can be made more comfortable with pillows.*

- Are you intending to leave the furniture outside all year? Is there a security issue? Heavy tables and benches, made from long-lasting hardwood, will last well outdoors, need little maintenance, and are more difficult to steal. Metal furniture must be well-painted to last and can deteriorate within a few years if not well manufactured. Lightweight aluminum furniture may be more water resistant but it is not always very strong.

- Is versatility an issue? Buying two small tables is a good option because you can place them around your yard and put them together for parties. Benches are more difficult to move than individual chairs but seat more people than chairs. Light backless benches are useful if you have children to feed. Rectangular tables are the most space-efficient but less friendly and more visually harsh than round ones.

- Are you concerned about sustainability and the materials in your furniture? Garden furniture is often made from tropical hardwoods. It can sometimes be very difficult to find out where the lumber is from, let alone if it was harvested responsibly. Look for wood from certification programs, such as those run by the international Forest Stewardship Council. Other options include bamboo and rattan, both of which are grown as grass and therefore promote regrowth and replacement.

Materials

Choosing chairs and tables for the yard is often driven by budget, although wrought-iron and wooden furniture styles are distinct and offer contrasting effects in the garden. Fortunately there is a range of prices in both materials, determined largely by the quality of the materials and construction.

WOOD

Versatile, natural, and strong, wood remains the most popular material for both garden chairs and tables. Teak is exotic and long-lasting, cedar is softer but durable, and pine—being inexpensive and easy to work and finish—is ideal for do-it-yourself projects. You can find alternatives from around the world at varying qualities and prices, but for long life outdoors, look for wood that is naturally oily or resinous, like teak or cedar, unless you plan to protect the furniture with paint or varnish.

You can shape wood into contemporary or classic styles; characteristic Adirondack and Colonial designs typify the material's versatility. Increasingly, designers are combining wood and metal, particularly brushed aluminum, for modern outdoor furniture suited to urban or suburban yards. You may want to use roundwood and driftwood for a more rustic feel— to bring the wilderness to cities.

Slatted seats are ideal and the most comfortable, especially if the slats are curved and thin enough to give a little. You'll probably need to use pillows for solid seats. Note that the wood will deteriorate quickly if water collects.

◀ A small wooden table and chairs are easily portable, allowing you to enjoy all parts of your garden, from shady secluded areas to sun-drenched lawns.

◀ ▲ Folding chairs (left) are a practical choice but do not require you to compromise on style. Adirondack chairs with their matching footrests (above) are a versatile choice, giving you the option of sitting or lounging.

Garden furniture tends to be oiled or varnished. Varnishing gives a high gloss and good protection but with time the surface coat may blister and crack. This can be repaired only by sanding and starting again. An oil finish, on the other hand, is built up gradually and you maintain the furniture by oiling every year or so, rubbing the oil into the grain with a nylon scouring pad. Alternatively you can just leave the wood to age on its own, with cracks appearing as it dries out.

▲ *Stackable chairs are a good alternative to folding ones. The metal frame makes stacking easy and is resistant to damage.*

▲ ▶ *The lounge chair (above) has a striking modern design and folds for easy storage. If you have a tree in your garden, install a bench (at right) around it to take advantage of the natural shade.*

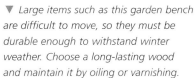

▼ *Large items such as this garden bench are difficult to move, so they must be durable enough to withstand winter weather. Choose a long-lasting wood and maintain it by oiling or varnishing.*

Wrought iron

With so much wood furniture in gardens and yards these days, wrought-iron can make a welcome change. Natural strength allows finer lines to form designs, compared to the heavier shapes and profiles that wooden pieces require. You also have a great opportunity to mix materials, adding canvas, pillows, or woven seats for extra comfort.

Wrought iron is the most commonly used metal for outdoor furniture. It is easy and inexpensive to manufacture, comes in many designs, and can be assembled at home with nuts and bolts. But be aware. These simple fittings often loosen with time, and wrought-iron tables and chairs may wobble. In some ways you're better off paying for welded furniture that lasts longer.

Over time, you will need to paint iron and non-stainless steel furniture, to inhibit rust and maintain it. The ends of rusting metal sections can become dangerously jagged. Tube steel furniture, which is often shaped by bending, is particularly vulnerable to deterioration from rust, especially if plastic or rubber "shoes" fall off. One solution is to fill the ends of the tubes with wooden bungs.

Aluminum is a good choice for garden furniture as it doesn't rust. When painted silver or another color, it can be attractive and not too expensive either.

▼ Wrought iron has the rustic charm of wood but without wood's characteristic bulky profile. This bench has been painted green to blend with the setting.

▲▼► The strength and flexibility of metals such as wrought iron and steel allow them to be crafted into a huge range of garden furniture designs.

◄ ▼ Traditionally ornate and delicate designs such as the love seat (left) still capture the imagination of many. Wrought iron is often combined with mosaics to create colorful and distinctive tables (below).

▼ Contemporary designs such as this aluminum chair are becoming more and more popular as garden furniture.

TABLE SIZES, SHAPES, AND CONSTRUCTION

Choosing a dining table size and shape that suits your preferred ways to dine outside depends on finding answers to critical questions.

Q Which shape is best for eating outdoors?

A This may depend on the shape and size of your eating area and how many guests you regularly invite. Rectangular tables, with one diner at each end and two or three along the sides, are the most space-efficient. Circular tables are more friendly because everyone faces each other, but there's a lot of wasted space in the center. Oval tables combine some of the qualities of circulars and rectangulars, but elliptical tables are even better, being long and thin with gentle curves along the sides that tighten at the ends. However, they are the most expensive to make and are often not available for purchase.

Q What size do tables need to be?

A On average, a rectangular table for eight people needs to be 86 inches (215cm) long and 36 inches (90cm) wide. Six people can sit around a table of similar width, but only 66 inches (165cm) long. You'll need a 50 inch (125cm) diameter circular table for six people, 54 inches (135cm) for seven, and 62 inches (155cm) for eight. Allow between 24 inches (60cm) and 26 inches (65cm) per person around the edge when estimating the size of an oval or elliptical table.

Q How high should a dining table be?

A The height of the table is determined by your chairs. The average height of dining tables tends to be about 29 inches (72.5cm), about 11 inches (27.5cm) higher than the average seat height of dining chairs. You need at least 6 inches (15cm) leg clearance between the seat height and the apron below the table top. Tables and chairs that are lower than average tend to give a more relaxed feel. You may be able to use these same chairs or benches around a lower coffee table.

◄ ▼ The chair (left) may look like wicker, but is actually a natural fiber that is smooth to the touch, so it won't snag clothes. The intricately woven seat of the chair (below) is balanced by the sculptural rattan frame.

RATTAN, BAMBOO, AND WICKER

These lightweight alternatives to wood— rattan, bamboo, and wicker—are natural materials that are harvested with ecological responsibility. They are comfortable and low cost, but are not renowned for durability. Furniture made from these materials lasts longest where it is not exposed to the elements.

The problem stems not so much from the materials themselves but the difficulty in joining the components. Bamboo is the most robust. Rattan, a type of cane usually grown in Southeast Asia, can become brittle and break. The same can be true of wicker, which is made from thin willow stems. Lightness, however, may be a significant advantage if you want to be able to move this type of furniture around and are happy to bring it indoors at the end of a day. There's plenty of resilience in these materials, often characterized by creaks as you sit down.

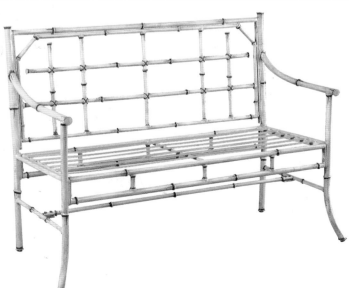

◄► A basic cane framework bench (left) can be customized for comfort with pillows. The classic deck chair design (right) still holds its own in the world of garden furniture. It is simple, comfortable, easy to store, and can be modified with a fabric to suit your taste.

A BENCH FOR ALL SEASONS

A bench, made from wrought iron or wood, and used on its own or beside a dining or coffee table, is a garden basic. When shortened, it becomes a dining chair with or without arms. Available in a huge range of styles, they are likely to be similar to those you use indoors. The classic bench can be further refined by gentle curving at the corners, or by including more severe bends in a love seat. Joined in sections, it becomes a tree seat. Without a back, the bench is a useful elongated stool, ideal for using on either side of a dining table. Other benches are combined with picnic tables or reserved for the children, but they tend to be heavier and more difficult to move.

Adirondack chairs, one of the more distinctive styles of outdoor furniture, are often made from cedar and with a fan-shaped back. They are usually designed as low armchairs, and are popular for their relaxed style, as well as their compatibility with many landscapes—from the veranda to the lake. They offer contrast with more upright director's chairs.

Folding chairs are a good option if you choose not to keep furniture outdoors all the time. These can be stacked in a corner or in a special box or used indoors. On cruise ships, the classic folding-design steamer chair is made from slatted wood and is a low lounger ideal for long, lazy days at sea.

Lounge chairs tend to be made either from wood or from a soft fabric on a metal, wood or plastic frame. Solid wood steamers look fantastic but are quite heavy and aren't that easily moved. You'll probably need to add pillows to make a wooden chair comfortable. The most comfortable lounge chairs are adjustable, so try before you buy to find the one that best suits your shape and body type.

▼ ▶ *Steamer chairs with footrests (right) are an adaptation of the deck chair. Their use on steamships in centuries past gives them a romantic appeal to many. Benches are attached to a table (below right) to reduce the risk of theft.*

◀ ▶ *A twisting adjustment of the classic bench design results in a unique piece (left). Benches (right) seat more people than individual chairs, so they are a good space-saving option for use at tables.*

VINTAGE STYLES

Outdoor furniture can be expensive. One option is to buy a second-hand piece and restore it. Due to the nature of life for outdoor furniture, not much survives to be sold secondhand, but it is relatively easy to restore if you find something you like. Strip off paint from metals using chemicals or a stripping wheel on a drill, then smooth with steel wool. Apply a rust-proof undercoat before the top coat. Rejuvenate natural wood by rubbing with a nylon scouring pad and oil and strip off paint with chemicals rather than abrasives, which tend to level all the interesting bruises and dents.

Look for various styles, new or secondhand, if you want to bring nostalgia to your yard. Steamer and

▼ ▶ A beautifully curved Lutyens bench (far right) makes an attractive focal point in a walled garden. If carrying drinks back and forth from the house spoils your lounging time, invest in a refrigerator or cooler disguised as a wooden chest (below).

Adirondack chairs have been popular for decades, and because they are made from wooden slats, they tend to be easy to repair if damaged. With their complicated curved backs, Lutyens wooden benches are more ornate, and give a finished look to your garden. Metal café tables, in French or Victorian styles, look good in the corner of a small deck or enigmatically alone beneath the drooping branches of a favorite tree. The fine lines of thin, old metal tables make them less conspicuous than wooden ones. Although formal in style, the curly, leaflike shapes complement a natural setting surprisingly well.

KEEPING FURNITURE SAFE

Outdoor furniture is annoyingly popular with thieves. Obviously heavier tables, chairs, and benches are more difficult to remove, but even that won't deter the most ambitious criminals. Anchoring items to the ground with brackets may help, and your supplier will be able to offer you various options.

Taking furniture indoors or storing the pieces in a locked shed or box are options that also protect it from the elements. If weather conditions are your only worry, consider furniture covers for individual items or for a group of table and chairs. Try to keep covered furniture ventilated to reduce the risk of damage from condensation.

BRINGING FOOD TO THE TABLE

Inevitably, you will need to bring some food and drinks to your outdoors table, even when you're enjoying a simple barbecue. Trays are the obvious solution, especially if you buy a folding stand so you won't

◀ ▲ You may need to protect your furniture from both thieves and the elements. You can use brackets to secure it to the ground (left), while covers will keep it safe from wind and rain (above).

have to move everything off the table when you struggle out with bowls of salad and liquid refreshment. A tray stand is easy to make with two X-sections joined with cross members and webbing.

A wheeled cart is also handy. To keep drinks cool outside, use a decorative cooler. Buy an umbrella for shade to keep everyone cool; choose one to fit in a hole in the table or one that stands on a block. There are even crane-like designs that suspend the umbrella on an extending arm.

▲ *If you don't have a conveniently located tree under which to site your garden dining table, opt for an umbrella that can be inserted into a hole in the center of the table to provide shade.*

▶ *A trolley is a great investment, allowing food and drink to be transported easily as well as acting as a small table.*

COMPARISON OF FURNITURE MATERIALS

Characteristics	Teak	Cedar	Oak	Pine	Wrought Iron	Aluminum	Steel	Canvas/Fabric
Durability	Good	Reasonable	Reasonable, but suffers in contact with metal and has open grain that can absorb water; needs finishing	Low; must be painted or varnished	Good, but needs repainting and joints can fail	Good	Needs protection	Canvas will deteriorate if allowed to stay wet; synthetic fabrics last well
Weight	Heavy	Light	Medium	Light	Can be heavy, but depends on size and design of piece	Light	Heavy	Light
Appearance	Solid; honey colored, ages gray; takes a sharp edge; not much resilience for comfort	Pale honey color, ages grays; wide, soft grain gives relaxed feel and good comfort	Lovely texture, and soon goes gray; interesting little cracks with age	Good for painting; knots must be sealed with shellac or they will weep	Classic old look that contrasts well with decking and complements natural setting	Perfect for contemporary setting; available in range of interesting designs	Fabulous handwrought designs available	Great colors and patterns available; usually held in wood or metal frame
Cost	Expensive	Medium	Medium	Low	Low to medium	Medium to expensive	Medium to expensive	Low

Hexagonal Tree Bench

YOU WILL NEED
Note: lengths will vary according to size of tree

Legs (A)
Twenty-four 20 in. (1400mm) 2 x 6 softwood

Lower rails (B)
Twelve 14 in. (350mm) 2 x 6 softwood

Seat supports (C)
Twelve 21 in. (530mm) 2 x 2 softwood

Seat slats (D)
Six 112 in. (2800) 2 x 6 softwood

Stakes (E)
One 72 in. (1400mm) 1 x 2 pressure-treated softwcod

Hardware and finishing
Seventy-two ½ in. (13mm) hardwood plugs

One hundred and seventy 2¼ in. (55mm) #10 galvanized screws

Twenty-four 3 in. (75mm) #10 galvanized screws for joining sections

Exterior wood glue

Paint, stain, or varnish of choice

Tools
Basic tool kit plus sliding bevel and power sander

B athed in dappled shade, a hexagonal bench constructed around a favorite tree offers a convenient place to sit, while framing the trunk and providing a special garden feature.

This piece is simple to make and can be adjusted to suit any size of tree, from a small flowering cherry to a mighty oak. A very big tree will obviously require a correspondingly large quantity of lumber, but most of us will have something more modest in mind. The main thing is that the principle—a modular bench built in six sections—remains the same, whatever the size of tree.

▶ *With its pleasing geometry, the tree bench makes an attractive garden feature and a pleasant place to sit, affording views all around the yard.*

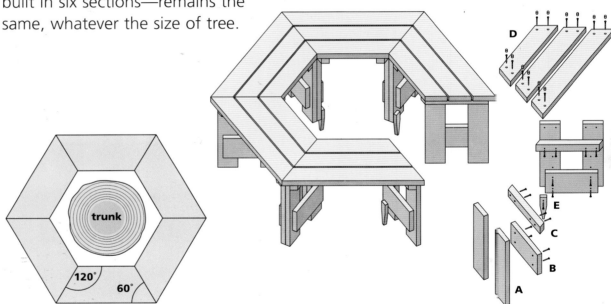

The angles made in the hexagon are shown in the diagram above. Leave a gap of between 6 and 12 inches (150–300mm) between the bark of the tree and the inside edge of the bench.

To calculate the size of the bench, draw a plan of the tree to scale, showing the diameter of the trunk, with six equally spaced lines radiating from the center. Mark a point about 6–12 inches (150–300mm) outward from the bark of the tree. Choose a point that will be comfortable for sitting. Too far leaves a large gap, too close offers no room for growth, and just right means you'll be able to lean back against the trunk.

The measurements given here suit a tree with a trunk that is about 21 inches (530mm) in diameter. They leave a gap of 6–12 inches (150–300mm) between the trunk and the inside edge of the bench, which means that the inside of each section is also about 21 inches (530mm) long.

1 Mark the position of the lower rails (B) on each leg (A). These should be placed 4 inches (100mm) from the bottom of each leg. Also mark the position of the seat supports (C), which will be attached flush with the top of each leg.

2 Drill and countersink the lower rails and glue and screw them to the legs. The legs should be set 6 inches (150mm) apart. Place these to one side while you prepare the seat supports.

3 Set a sliding bevel to 30 degrees and mark one end of each seat support (C). By angling the ends of the seat supports, you'll have a neater result at the front and back.

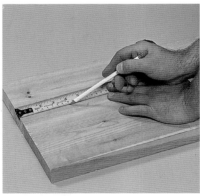

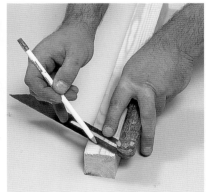

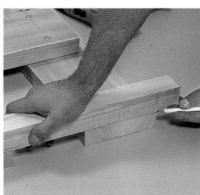
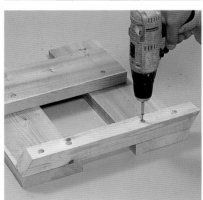

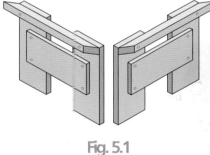

Fig. 5.1

4 Cut the angle and position the seat support on the assembled leg section to determine the length of the support and where you have to make the other angled cut. Once again, mark with a sliding bevel, making sure the angle is parallel to the one at the other end.

5 The angles might look a little strange at this stage, but it works out once the bench has been assembled. Cut the remaining seat supports and attach them to the other leg sections in the same way, but alternating their direction so you arrive at six pairs of leg sections as shown in fig. 5.1. You can speed up the operation by using a template to mark all the parts.

6 Mark and cut the innermost seat slats (D). The inside edge for this size of seat is 21 inches (530mm) long, diverging by 30 degrees to the outside edge (fig. 6.1). Lay out the wood for the other seat slats, either on the ground or on the bench, with ¾ inch (20mm) spacers between the slats. Using a straightedge set along the angled ends of the innermost slat as a guide, mark the angle of cut on the remaining slats. Cut to size.

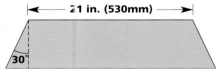

21 in. (530mm)

30°

Fig. 6.1

ADDING A BACKREST

More experienced woodworkers might like to add a back to their bench. This is a complicated business, as the slope of the back toward the tree as well as the upward taper in each section combine to give tricky compound angles! In addition you'll require a circular saw to cut long miters and the skill to use it.

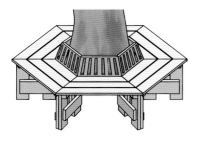

STRENGTHENING SHELF

A shelf makes a useful addition to the bench and has the added plus of increasing its structural strength. Measure and cut additional seat slats and screw these to the top edge of the lower rails of some or all of the seat sections. In order to avoid awkward drilling operations, these are best fixed in place before the seats slats are glued and screwed into position.

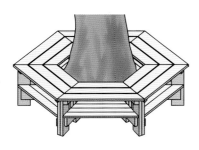

7 Lay out the cut slats on the leg sections, spacing them ¾ inch (20mm) apart, and mark the drill positions. Drill holes for the screws and oversize holes for the plugs. Screw and glue the seat slats to the seat supports and glue in the plugs.

9 Place the sections in position around the tree and carry out any necessary leveling of the ground to ensure the sections align correctly. Assemble the bench by clamping the leg sections together two at a time. Screw together using four 3 inch (75mm) screws, one at the top and one at the bottom of both inside and outside legs. Continue around until all sections are joined (fig. 9.1).

8 Clean up the surface of the slats and the plugs with a power sander and remove the sharp outside edges of the slats by beveling with a block plane. Repeat the assembly and cleaning for all six sections of the seat. Apply the finish of your choice.

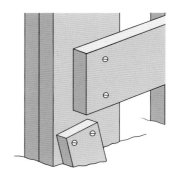

10 Cut six 12 inch (300mm) stakes from the treated softwood (E) to resemble tent pegs and use them to fix the bench in position, wedging them up against the legs. Drive each stake 8 inches (200mm) into the ground with a hammer, then screw it to the leg section (fig. 10.1).

Fig. 9.1

Fig. 10.1

Simply Designed Chair

Woodworkers consider chairs among the hardest pieces to make: they must be as robust as they are handsome, and they include complex angled joints. Strength is particularly important for outdoor furniture because of the constant fluctuations in temperature and moisture levels, and also because it often sits on ground that isn't quite level.

This chair is made from wide slats and has a gently sloping back for comfort. It is both attractive and sturdy, with a solidity that contrasts nicely with the organic backdrop of a garden or complements a contemporary setting. Notice how the tapered legs lighten its appearance without any loss of strength.

► *Solid-looking but with clean lines, this chair will suit a range of garden locations, from a paved terrace near the house to a more informal position such as beside a rustic path or on a lawn.*

Unlike most garden chairs, this project is relatively easy to build. It requires no complicated joints or any specialized tools. Like the Versatile Garden Table (page 72), it is built around an underframe. If you have difficulty finding 3 x 3 lumber for the legs (dressed size 2½ x 2½), buy 4 x 4 and have it planed to size by your supplier.

1 Cut the front and back legs to length (A). Measure 10 inches (255mm) up from the bottom of the legs and make a mark. This is the position of the underframe rails (B). Make sure the distance below the rail is the same on the front and back legs.

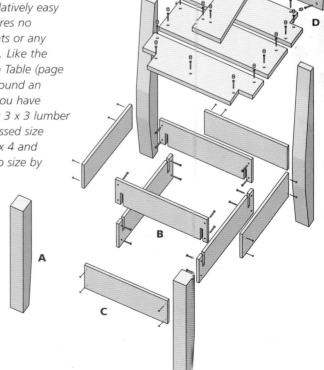

2 Measure 1⅞ inches (45mm) from the edge on one face of the leg and mark the spot. Join this line to the mark made to locate the underframe rails. This is the lower leg taper line. Use a square to mark it across the end and up the adjacent side and cut the taper with a table saw or circular saw. Repeat on the remaining three legs. Now mark a similar taper for the sloping back on the upper portion of the rear legs. This time the taper runs for a length of 22½ inches (570mm) and again tapers to a width of 1⅞ inches (45mm) at the top of the leg (fig. 2.1). Clean up the rough edges with a plane and sanding block.

3 The inside of the legs are screwed to an underframe to give the chair rigidity. To make the underframe, use halving joints as shown in the Dovecote project (page 140). The underframe rails overlap the legs by about 1⅞ inch (45mm). Clamp the front and back underframe rails together to mark the overlap.

4 Use one of the rails to mark the width of the halving joint on a pair of underframe rails. Mark lines down the faces of the rails to a point that's half the rail's width. Repeat this process for the other underframe rails. Marking and cutting the joints together guarantees that they will be in the same position.

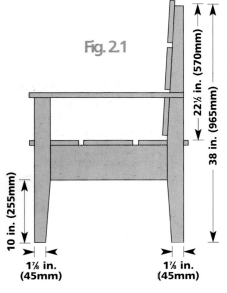

Fig. 2.1

22½ in. (570mm)

38 in. (965mm)

10 in. (255mm)

1⅞ in. (45mm)

1⅞ in. (45mm)

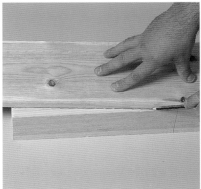

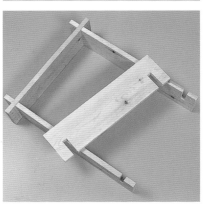

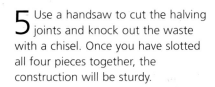

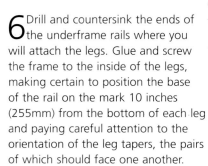

5 Use a handsaw to cut the halving joints and knock out the waste with a chisel. Once you have slotted all four pieces together, the construction will be sturdy.

6 Drill and countersink the ends of the underframe rails where you will attach the legs. Glue and screw the frame to the inside of the legs, making certain to position the base of the rail on the mark 10 inches (255mm) from the bottom of each leg and paying careful attention to the orientation of the leg tapers, the pairs of which should face one another.

TAPERED LINES

Another way to lighten the chair's appearance is by tapering both inside faces of the legs so you can see the taper from the front as well as the sides. For a more ornate effect, you could buy some small wooden balls and screw them to the bottom of the legs as "feet."

7 Once the glue on the underframe has set, which usually means leaving it overnight, attach the fascia rails (C). Glue and nail them to the ends of the underframe rails to both hide the underframe and to make the chair more substantial (fig. 7.1).

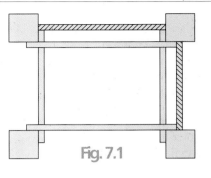

Fig. 7.1

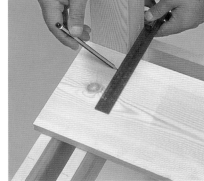

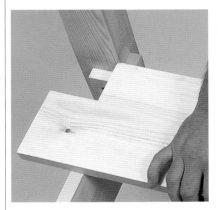

8 Let the glue set overnight and then attach the seat slats (D) to the underframe. You will have to notch the back and front slats around the legs. To mark the notch width, place the front and back slats on the underframe and use the legs as guides.

9 Mark each notch 3¼ inches (82mm) deep with a square, then cut it out with a jigsaw, always cutting on the outside of the line. Check the fit of each slat as you cut it. Note that the front and back slats will overhang the legs by about ¾ inch (20mm) in both directions.

10 Once the front and back seat slats are in place, position the center slat so that the gaps between them are equal. Check to see they are straight, then use a square to mark lines showing where the fascia rails end below the slats. Using these lines as guides, mark the holes for screwing the slats into the fascia rails. Drill countersinking holes no more than ½ inch (13mm) into the slats.

ARE YOU SITTING COMFORTABLY?

You'll need a cushion or cushions to make the flat seat comfortable, or alternatively, you can shape the seat. To do this, cut curves along the top edges of the side underframe rails and the side fascia rails. You'll need to do this before putting the chair together, of course, and you may prefer to use narrower seat slats, which will follow the curve more effectively.

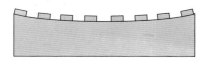

11 Screw the seat slats to the fascia rails and glue the hardwood plugs in place. Make sure the grain of the plugs aligns with that of the surrounding wood and gently tap the plugs in with a hammer. Once the glue has set, cut off any excess with a chisel or small finish saw. The best way to do this is to leave each plug slightly raised above the slat and then sand it flush.

12 Attach the lowest back slat, clamping it in place while you screw it to the back leg. Position it so that the upper edge of the slat is exactly level with the top of the front legs.

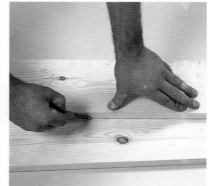

14 Use a straightedge to mark the taper on the outer edge of the arms and then cut them with a handsaw. The taper should be 1 inch (25mm) only. It's best to do this after you've cut out the notch because you can put the arm in the final position and get a good idea of how the taper will look (fig. 14.1).

13 With the lowest back slat in place, mark and cut out the notches on the arms (E) to fit around the back legs. Mark the locations for the holes you'll use to screw the arms to the back slats and the tops of the front legs.

Fig. 14.1

CUTOUTS ADD INTEREST

For a more ornate effect, cut out shapes in the back slats with a jigsaw or a scrolling jigsaw. Traditional shapes include diamonds and hearts. As always, drill pilot holes to give the saw blade access.

SHAPING THE BACK

To change the feel of the chair, consider cutting a curve along the top back slat. For a contemporary look, the curve can be very simple; a more ornate curve will give a more rustic look. You can also repeat the curve on the ends of the arms and along the front edge of the seat or fascia.

15 Drill, glue and screw the arms to the back slat and the tops of the front legs. The holes at the front of the arms will be plugged, so use a counterbore bit or, if that's not possible, drill the plug holes first—otherwise it will be difficult to keep the drill bit steady. Make sure the holes align and are ⅜ inch (9mm) deep.

16 Drill and screw the two remaining back slats into position. The middle slat sits on the arms, hiding the screws, but you'll need to use a spacer to position the top slat. Clamp the slats to hold them steady while you screw them in place.

17 Glue and tap in the remaining plugs. Make sure the grain of the plugs aligns with that of the surrounding wood and gently tap them in with a hammer. Once the glue has set, cut off any excess with a chisel, utility knife or small finish saw,   then sand flush.

18 Finally, sand the entire chair lightly to remove any marking lines. For a professional finish, sand the arms on all the edges and corners with medium to fine sandpaper. After brushing off the sawdust, the chair is ready to oil, varnish or paint.

Versatile Garden Table

Here's an easy-to-make low table that matches the Simply Designed Chair (page 66). It shares some of the construction details and techniques but is even quicker to put together.

It may look big, but don't let that scare you: a table is one of the best projects for a novice woodworker. You only need to attach four legs to an underframe and add a top. In this case, because the table is for garden use, we're using a slatted top, which allows rainwater to drip away between the slats. The table can be made from any grade of pine or spruce, but if you intend to finish it in a transparent varnish, you might want to choose best quality clear (that is, knot-free) pine.

► *The finished table makes a useful and attractive addition to an outdoor living space such as a deck or patio, especially when accompanied by the matching chair on page 66.*

The techniques used to make this table are very similar to those for the Simply Designed Chair (page 66). As with the chair, the assembly is built around an underframe constructed with halving joints.

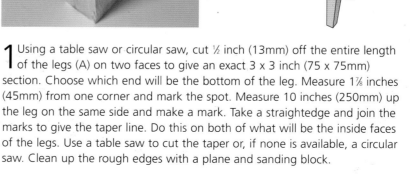

Fig. 1.1

10 in
(250mm)

1⅞ in
(45mm)

1 Using a table saw or circular saw, cut ½ inch (13mm) off the entire length of the legs (A) on two faces to give an exact 3 x 3 inch (75 x 75mm) section. Choose which end will be the bottom of the leg. Measure 1⅞ inches (45mm) from one corner and mark the spot. Measure 10 inches (250mm) up the leg on the same side and make a mark. Take a straightedge and join the marks to give the taper line. Do this on both of what will be the inside faces of the legs. Use a table saw to cut the taper or, if none is available, a circular saw. Clean up the rough edges with a plane and sanding block.

2 The underframe is held together with halving joints located 1½ inches (38mm) from the board ends. Clamp both side rails together before marking the position of the joints; do the same for the end and central rails. Use a ruler and pencil or a marking gauge to mark the depth of the joints to half the width of the boards.

3 Cut down the joint lines with a handsaw and use a chisel and mallet to remove the waste. You can work on one rail at a time or in pairs, as shown. Cut down from one side and then the other to reduce the risk of splintering.

Fig. 4.1

4 Assemble the underframe as shown in fig. 4.1 and glue and screw the legs to it with two screws per side, ensuring the tops of the legs align with the top of the underframe. The screws will be covered by the fascia rails so they don't need plugging.

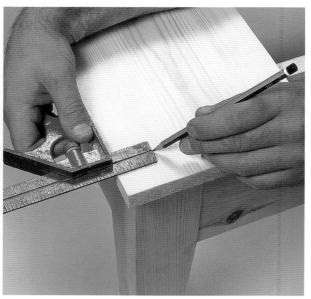

5 Glue and nail the fascia rails (C and D) to the ends of the cross rails, sinking the nailheads below the surface with a nail set. Be careful not to damage the surface of the wood as you knock the nails home. You can fill these holes later with wood putty or a home-made filler made of white glue mixed with sawdust.

6 Lay out the slats for the top (E) separated by ¾ inch (19mm) spacers, ensuring that the overhang is the same at each end. Using a long straightedge, mark a line as a positioning guide for the screws that will be used to attach the top to the fascia rails. Space the screws evenly, the same distance from the edge of each board.

7 Mark the position of each drill hole exactly; using a small cross to identify these points will enable you to be precise.

MAKING YOUR OWN PLUGS

Instead of buying wooden plugs, you can make your own with a plug cutter—a sort of hollow drill bit that's shaped like an apple corer. For the best results use a drill press or set the drill in a stand, with the wood held firmly. The best cutters are tapered to make plugs that fit tightly. This tool is ideal if you want to use a specific type of wood to match a project.

HINGED TOP

One variation on this design has the table top hinged rather than fixed, with two cross members holding the slats in position. In this arrangement you would omit the central underframe rail and put a plywood base in the underframe, which would then act as a storage compartment. Scalloped fascia rails are another decorative alternative.

8 Drill pilot holes for the screws all the way through each board. Use a ½ inch (13mm) counterbore bit to drill ⅜ inch (9mm) deep holes for the plugs. Screw the boards to the rails.

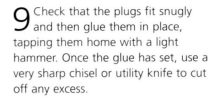

10 Use a block plane or sanding block to bevel the sharp edges on the table top.

9 Check that the plugs fit snugly and then glue them in place, tapping them home with a light hammer. Once the glue has set, use a very sharp chisel or utility knife to cut off any excess.

11 Sand the entire top, including the plugs, with a sanding block or a power sander. Also sand the legs and fascia rails lightly to remove any marking lines. Wipe off the sawdust with a damp rag before applying the desired finish.

Mosaic Table

YOU WILL NEED

Legs (A)
Four 30 in. (750mm) 3 x 3 softwood

Base support (B)
One 20 x 20 in. (500 x 500mm) piece
of ¾ in. (18mm) marine plywood

Skirt pieces (C)
Four 20 in. (500mm) 2 x 6 softwood

Circular table top (D)
One 48 x 48 in. (1220 x 1220mm) piece
of ¾ in. (18mm) marine plywood

Colored tiles (E)
Sufficient to cover an area of
11 sq. feet (0.9m²)

Hardware and finishing
Sixteen 2 in. (50mm) #10 galvanized
screws

Eight 2½ in. (65mm) #10 galvanized
screws

Four 1¼ in. (30mm) #10 galvanized screws

Wood filler

Exterior wood glue

Polyurethane sealant

Tile adhesive

Exterior grout

Wood preservative, paint, stain, varnish

Tools
Basic tool kit plus mallet, tile pliers,
grouting float and vise

M osaic is a fantastic material for brightening any garden and a huge range of tile colors is available. You can combine tiles in an infinite number of patterns, which gives you great opportunities to create simple projects. This table is easy to make, with clean lines that won't conflict with the mosaic surface.

The table is made from a combination of softwood and marine plywood, which is treated to be water resistant. The size of the top is determined by how many people you want to seat: the diameter here is 40 inches (1000mm), which is ample for four and possibly five.

The legs and skirt of the table can be stained, varnished or painted to match the mosaic design on the top.

▶ *The mosaic table brings color and pattern to a patio area and makes an arresting and original focal point.*

1 Mark a notch in the top of each leg (A) measuring 1 inch (25mm) wide by ¾ inch (19mm) deep, using a combination square or marking gauge. These notches will house the corners of the base support (B).

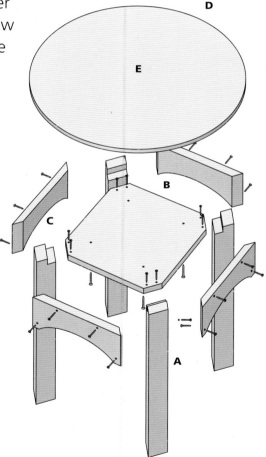

The construction is simplicity itself: four sturdy legs (A) are joined to the base support (B) with a simple lap joint, and the whole assembly is reinforced by the skirt pieces (C). If you have difficulty finding 3 x 3 lumber for the legs (dressed size 2½ x 2½ inches), cut and plane down a length of 4 x 4 to the required dimensions, or ask your lumber dealer to do it.

2 Holding a leg against a bench hook or in a vise, cut across the grain with a tenon saw, keeping to the waste side of the notch mark. Stop just short of the second mark, which is at right angles to the first.

3 Remove the waste with a chisel and mallet. Make sure the grain runs straight along the leg or you may accidentally chop out too much wood, reducing the bonding face and weakening the joint. Cut out the notches on all four legs.

4 Measure and mark the base support (E) 1½ inches (40mm) along both sides from each corner and use a straightedge to join up the marks. Cut off the resulting triangles with a handsaw. This leaves a diagonal on each corner that will fit neatly in the notches cut in the legs.

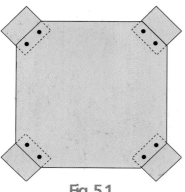

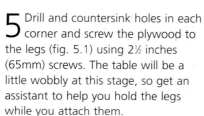

Fig. 5.1

5 Drill and countersink holes in each corner and screw the plywood to the legs (fig. 5.1) using 2½ inches (65mm) screws. The table will be a little wobbly at this stage, so get an assistant to help you hold the legs while you attach them.

6 Position the skirt pieces (C) to mark the location of the miter joints. Hold the skirt piece so its side and ends align with the side and ends of the base support as shown and mark the position of the leg at each end. Mark and cut the pieces one at a time, as the angles formed by the legs may vary slightly from one to another.

PLANING THE LEGS

You can alter the shape of the legs by planing a bevel on the two outside edges of the skirt pieces. How much wood you remove depends on the effect you want to achieve, from a subtle beveled edge to a greatly squared-off face. The best way to do this is to hold the legs firmly in a vise, before they are attached to the base support.

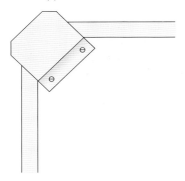

REPOSITIONING THE LEGS

For an alternative look, change the way the legs are positioned. Place them so the corners, rather than the flat sides, point out. You can bevel the edges, as described above, to create an octagonal shape. Notice that with this method you don't need to miter the ends of the skirt pieces, which makes the project simpler if you don't own a miter saw.

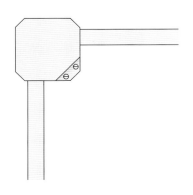

7 Use a combination square to mark the 45 degree miter on the edges of the skirt pieces and join the marks across the faces. You can cut these miters by hand, but using a miter block or a miter saw makes the job simpler, speedier and more accurate.

9 Clean up the skirt pieces with sandpaper. Drill and countersink the holes for screwing the skirt pieces to the legs and the base support. Drill the two holes for the legs diagonally at an angle so the screws go through the end of the skirt piece (fig. 9.1). Screw the skirt pieces to the table and make sure you fill the countersunk screw heads with wood glue before applying wood preservative or varnish to finish.

8 Make a template for marking the curve in the skirt pieces. Make a mark ½ inch (13mm) from the top edge of one component halfway along its length. Position a thin piece of flexible batten along the top edge of the component and clamp at both ends. Push the batten at the center until it reaches the mark. Clamp the batten in place and draw around it to mark the curve. Cut this with a jigsaw. Once you are happy with the curve, use it as a template for marking the other skirt pieces.

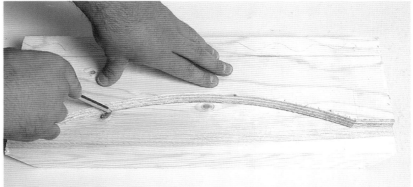

10 Now turn to the table top (D). Locate the center of the plywood and tap in a nail at this point. Attach a pencil to the nail by a length of string measuring 20 inches (500mm). Use this to draw a circle on the plywood with a diameter of 40 inches (1000mm).

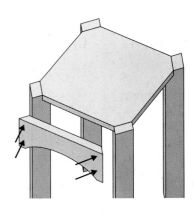

Fig. 9.1

ROUND LEGS

For a more rustic look use 3 inches (75mm) diameter round wood from a garden center. Notch the table top (see Step 4), but flatten the sides where the skirts will be attached. Experiment with how much or how little of the legs you show; the larger the notch for the top, the stronger the table.

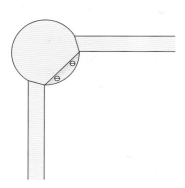

11 Cut out the circle with a jigsaw, trying to keep tearing to a minimum. This happens most at the top of the cut, so use this side for the top of the table, which will be covered with mosaic tiles. Tearing occurs more when you cut into the grain, rather than with it.

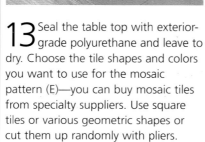

13 Seal the table top with exterior-grade polyurethane and leave to dry. Choose the tile shapes and colors you want to use for the mosaic pattern (E)—you can buy mosaic tiles from specialty suppliers. Use square tiles or various geometric shapes or cut them up randomly with pliers.

12 Drill four holes halfway along each side of the base support and screw to the table top from underneath using 1¼ inches (30mm) screws. Draw your pattern on the table top in pencil. Go over the lines with dark marker pen that will show through any sealer and adhesive (fig. 12.1).

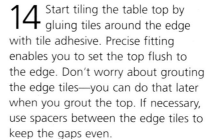

14 Start tiling the table top by gluing tiles around the edge with tile adhesive. Precise fitting enables you to set the top flush to the edge. Don't worry about grouting the edge tiles—you can do that later when you grout the top. If necessary, use spacers between the edge tiles to keep the gaps even.

Fig. 12.1

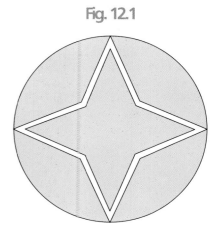

BANDED EDGING

As an alternative to tiling the edge of the table top, you can apply a thin wooden or aluminum band. Both types of band are available from home stores and are easy to bend and attach. Gently bend the band to shape and screw it in place. For a really neat joint, cut the band at an angle to produce a scarf joint. If you are using aluminum, make sure you clean up any sharp edges or points with a file.

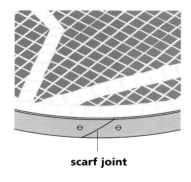

scarf joint

15 Mosaic tiles are often supplied in strips. Lay the tiles against the pattern and mark where any need to be cut.

16 The tiles are best cut using tile nippers or pliers. They should break easily enough, but you may need to cut them back gradually to reach your desired angle and shape.

17 Once you have laid out the lines that make up the star, simply fill in between the points. Most of this can be done with whole tiles, but you will need to nip some to fit.

18 Fill the gaps between the tiles with grout, using a rubber grouting float to push the creamy liquid into the gaps. Wipe away any excess grout with a damp rag. Once it has dried, buff off the film it leaves with a soft cloth.

Lounge Chair

Lounging in the garden is one of summer's luxuries, although this chair could be used all year round in a sunroom. It is designed as a day bed—to raise your upper body for reading, chatting, or snoozing—and is best used with pillows or a mattress for comfort.

The concept of a tilting section sounds complicated, but in fact this chair is relatively simple to make. You can finish it with stain and varnish or paint, although for indoor use it won't need much weatherproofing. Instead it can be allowed to age gradually as it becomes a favorite place to settle.

▶ *A very gentle curve along the sides of the underframe adds flair, giving the lounge chair a more sophisticated look.*

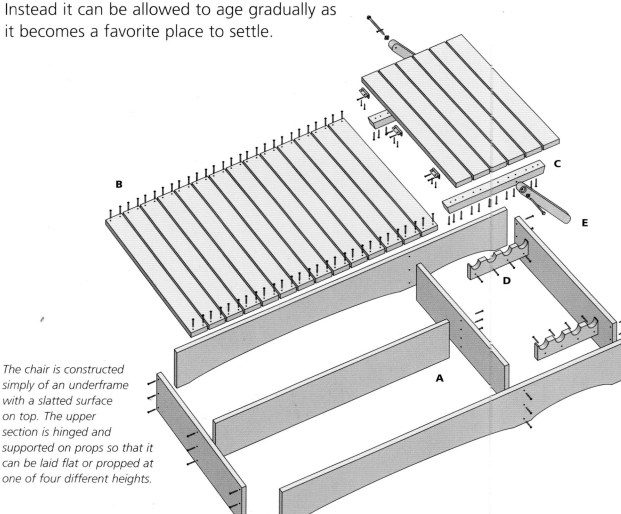

The chair is constructed simply of an underframe with a slatted surface on top. The upper section is hinged and supported on props so that it can be laid flat or propped at one of four different heights.

1 Take one of the side pieces of the underframe (A) (fig. 5.1). Measure 56 inches (1400mm) from one end (P) and mark this point (Q) to indicate the position of the horizontal central divider. Mark a line (S) 2 inches (50mm) to the left and another (T) 2 inches (50mm) to the right of this point. Mark a line (U) 4 inches (100mm) from end P of the frame piece and another (V) 4 inches (100mm) from end R. Find the midpoint between marks U and S. Measure and mark 1½ inches (40mm) up from this point. Repeat at the midpoint between marks T and V. Clamp one end of the flexible batten at point U and hold the other loosely at point S.

2 Find the center of the batten and gently push it up to the mark at the midpoint between U and S. Clamp the batten at S so that it forms a 1½ inch (40mm) deep curve. Using a sharp pencil, draw the curve along the inner edge of the batten. Repeat at the other end between points T and V and draw the curve there.

3 Cut the curves with a jigsaw and smooth out any irregularities with sandpaper. Using this side piece as a template, copy the curves onto the other side of the underframe. Cut and sand this side.

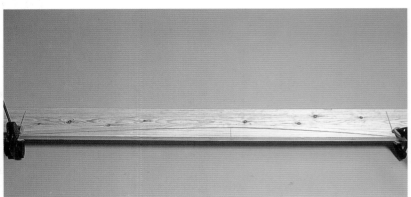

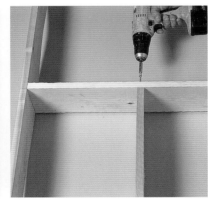

4 Drill all the underframe components for assembly as shown in the exploded diagram. Use a T-square to ensure the pieces are square to each other as you drill the holes. The pieces are joined with three screws per joint, drilled about 1 inch (25mm) in from the top and bottom, with another screw in the center.

5 Start by screwing the corner joints, and then move to the central dividers. The construction is reasonably strong at this stage but will be greatly reinforced by the slatted surface. Once the underframe is screwed together (fig. 5.1), check that the corners are square before fitting the slats.

P–Q = 56 in. (1400mm)
S–Q = 2 in. (50mm)
Q–T = 2 in. (50mm)
P–U = 4 in. (100mm)
V–R = 4 in. (100mm)

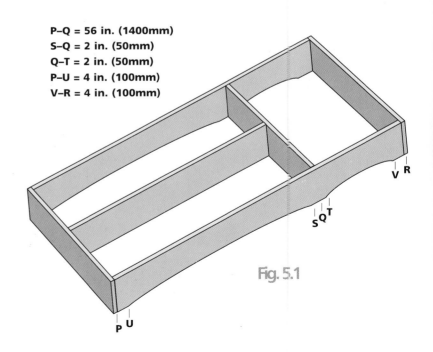

Fig. 5.1

REPETITIVE DRILLING

Drilling holes in the ends of the slats is exactly the sort of task that can be accelerated by using an improvised jig in a drill press. The fence X acts as a stop, ensuring that each hole is drilled exactly the same distance from the end of each slat. The guide blocks Y and Z are clamped to the fence and positioned about 2½ inches (88mm) farther apart than the width of the slat and equidistant from the drill center. The slats are pushed first against one block and drilled, then against the other and drilled, ensuring precise and even spacing without the bother of measuring and marking each individual slat.

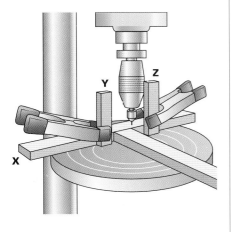

6 Sand the ends of the slats (B) smooth. Then drill and countersink two holes at each end of each slat, the same distance from the ends and the edges (see sidebar for a speedier way to do this). Attach the first slat with its top edge flush with the horizontal central divider. You can also attach this slat to the divider for added strength.

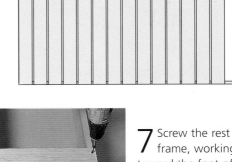

Fig. 7.1

7 Screw the rest of the slats to the frame, working from the divider toward the foot of the chair and using a spacer to keep the gaps consistent. In the 14-plus-6-slat bench here (fig. 7.1), we have ½ inch (12mm) gaps, but depending on the exact dimensions of your wood you might need greater or lesser spacing: test first in a dry run and calculate the exact gap width required.

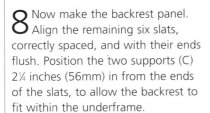

8 Now make the backrest panel. Align the remaining six slats, correctly spaced, and with their ends flush. Position the two supports (C) 2¼ inches (56mm) in from the ends of the slats, to allow the backrest to fit within the underframe.

9 Drill and countersink equally spaced holes into the supports. Screw the supports to the slats through the countersunk holes, once again using the spacer to keep the gaps consistent.

WHEELS IN MOTION

You can make the lounge chair more mobile by adding wheels or casters. The simplest way to do this is to bolt wooden wheels to the frame of the chair. Alternatively, you could glue and screw corner blocks inside the framework and screw metal casters to the base of the blocks.

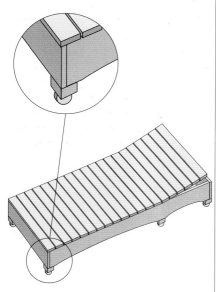

10 Use a spade bit to drill four 1½ inch (40mm) holes along the centerline of the plywood prop support piece (D). Position one hole near each end of the plywood and space the others evenly between them. Drill and countersink holes for screwing the supports to the framework, one on either side of each of the larger holes as shown below.

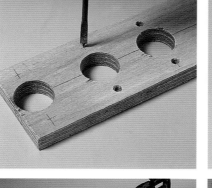

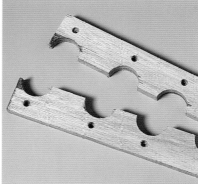

11 Cut the piece in half down the centerline to create two notched prop supports that will hold the backrest props in position.

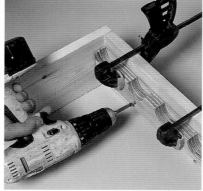

12 Glue and screw the prop supports to the underframe 1½ inches (40mm) below the top edge of the frame. It's always a good idea to clamp each piece in place before driving home the screws, but make sure you protect the outside of the frame from marking by the clamp heads.

13 Use a compass to mark a semicircle on the wider face at both ends of each backrest prop (E), then cut around the marks with a coping saw. This gives them a rounded shape so the props can pivot.

HANDY SHELF

For the ultimate in lounging, you can attach a shelf for drinks, sunglasses, and books to the side of the lounge chair. This is simply a piece of wood attached by a couple of shaped wooden brackets or purchased metal ones. Finish it in a contrasting color to highlight exactly where you'd like your drink delivered!

front view

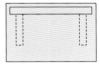

side view

location

14 Drill the wider face at one end of each prop for lag screws. Counterbore for the washers so that the screws don't undo themselves when you move the props and also so that you can assemble the props with a spanner wrench.

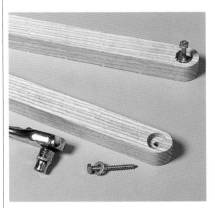

15 Lay the backrest face down on the lower part of the chair and align the two edges to be joined; that is, the bottom slat of the backrest with the top slat of the main section. With an assistant holding the two pieces firmly in place, screw three butt hinges to the edges of the two slats, one at each end and one in the center. Make sure the backrest moves easily on the hinges.

16 With the backrest still folded face-down on the lower section of the chair, attach a support prop to the outer edge of one of the backrest supports at the center of the fourth slat from the hinges.

17 Once you're satisfied with the operation of the prop on one side, attach its twin on the other side. Fill the screw holes with filler and, when dry, apply wood preservative and your choice of paint, stain, and/or varnish to the chair.

Curved Back Bench

YOU WILL NEED

Back legs (A)
Six 36 in. (910mm) 1 x 4 softwood

Front and back seat rails (B)
Two 59 in. (1500mm) 1 x 4 softwood

Top rail (C)
One 59 in. (1500mm) 1 x 8 softwood with a curved top that narrows to 4 in. (100mm) at the ends, cut using the batten method described on page 83

Armrest supports (D)
Two 20 in. (500mm) 1 x 2 softwood

End and central seat rails (E)
Three 20 in. (500mm) 1 x 4 softwood

Front legs (F)
Six 24½ in. (620mm) 1 x 4 softwood

Seat slats (G)
Three 65 in. (1650mm) 1 x 8 softwood

Back batten (H)
One 59 in. (1500mm) 1 x 2 softwood

Thin back slats (I)
Four 24 in. (600mm) 1 x 4 softwood

Wide back slats (J)
Five 24 in. (600mm) 1 x 8 softwood

Capping rail (K)
One 72 in. (1830mm) 1 x 4 softwood

Armrests (L)
Two 24¾ in. (630mm) 1 x 4 softwood

Hardware and finishing

Fifty-four 1¼ in. (30mm) #8 galvanized screws

Twenty 1½ in. (40mm) #10 galvanized screws

Thirty 2 in. (50mm) #10 galvanized screws

Eighteen 1½ in. (40mm) galvanized finishing nails

Sixty-three ½ in. (13mm) hardwood plugs

Exterior wood glue

Wood preservative, paint, stain, varnish

Tools
Basic tool kit plus sliding bevel, mallet

The solidity required of a bench is traditionally achieved by joining the cross rails to the legs with a mortise and tenon joint. These come in many varieties, but all demand very accurate layout and time-consuming, careful cutting out. For the bench built here, we've devised an alternative method which involves laminating, or gluing, the legs together in three layers, first cutting notches in the central lamination. These notches then form the mortises for the end rails. The seat is pitched back at a 5 degree angle to make it more comfortable, but this isn't as complicated as you might think. The front legs remain vertical, which means that the end rail, armrest, and armrest support join the front legs at a corresponding 5 degree angle. Everything else is cut at right angles.

▶ *The clean lines and elegant proportions of this bench work well in a smart urban setting, but would equally suit a formal area in a country garden.*

This project uses barefaced tenon joints to join the components of the bench securely together, which means you don't need to spend hours crafting mortise and tenon joints.

Fig. 1.1

5°

5°

5°

90°

2 Measure 13½ inches (343mm) from the bottom of the central section of one back leg and cut a 3½ inch (90mm) wide by 1⅜ inch (35mm) deep notch for the end seat rail. Measure 21 inches (533mm) from the same point and cut a 1½ inch (38mm) by 1⅜ inch (35mm) deep notch for the armrest support.

3 Use the notched leg section as a template for marking the other central lamination. Cut out the notches with a handsaw, chopping out the waste with a chisel and mallet.

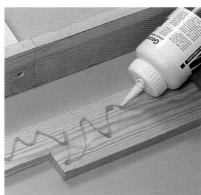

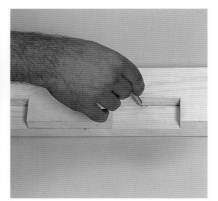

1 Measure, mark and cut a 5 degree angle in the tops and bottoms of all six back leg sections (A) so that the legs sit solidly on the ground when tilted back. Cut a similar angle in the tops of the front legs and in one end of both armrest supports (D) and end seat rails (E).

Drill, glue and screw the inner back leg section to the back seat rail (B) and top rail (C), using a 1⅜ inch (35mm) thick spacer to position the rails centrally on the leg. The top rail is flush with the top of the leg, and the back seat rail is positioned 13½ inches (343mm) from the foot of the leg.

4 Glue and clamp the central, notched laminations for the back legs to the inner laminations, taking care to line the sections up precisely. Drill and screw together. You can't go back now, because the central laminations cover the screws that hold the inner laminations to the seat rail and top back rail.

5 Spread glue into the "mortises" for the armrest supports (D) and end seat rails (E).

6 Screw the drilled armrest supports and end seat rails into the mortises, checking to see that they are square. Repeat for the other back leg. Once the glue has set, lift the back assembly and rest it against a wall so that it is upright with the feet flat on the ground.

USING CONVENTIONAL MORTISE AND TENON JOINTS

As mentioned earlier, the mortise and tenon joint is the traditional choice when you are making a bench or chair. If you have the experience, you can cut this joint with hand tools or a router. The s mpler joints used in this project are known as barefaced tenons because the full width and thickness of the tenon fits into the mortise.

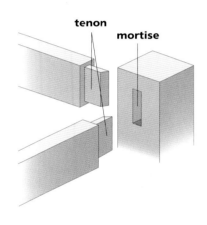

tenon

mortise

7 Next, offer up the central front leg laminations (F) to the back assembly and mark the notch positions for the end seat rails and the armrest supports. Cut out the notches as before to a maximum depth of 1⅜ inch (35mm). Drill, glue and screw the inner front leg sections to the front seat rail (B) using a 1⅜ inch (35mm) thick spacer to position the rail centrally on the leg. Glue and screw the central laminations in place, as you did for the back sections. You can then join the front and back halves together by screwing the end seat rails and the armrest supports to the mortises in the front legs.

8 Attach the outer leg laminations (A and F) to the back and front legs by gluing, clamping and screwing them in place. Counter-bore the holes using a ½ inch (13mm) spade bit to a depth of ⅜ inch (10mm). When the glue has set, plane the edges of the laminated sections absolutely flush.

10 Once the glue in the legs has set, attach the seat to the underframe. Cut notches in the front and rear seat slats (G) to fit around the legs, allowing the slats to overhang the front and rear seat rails and the side rails by ¾ inch (19mm) (see fig. 10.1). With front and rear slats in place, position the middle slat equally between them and check to see that they all line up and fit correctly.

9 Drill and screw the central seat rail (E) to the front and back seat rails. Counterbore using a ½ inch (13mm) spade bit to a depth of ⅜ inch. The holes will be filled with hardwood plugs at a later stage.

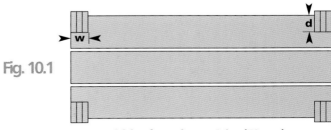

Fig. 10.1

width of notch w = 3 in. (72mm)
depth of notch d = 4¼ in. (104mm)

CURVING THE SEAT

Although we've inclined the back of the bench to make it comfortable, gently curving the seat boards will make it even more ergonomic. All you have to do is cut a gentle curve along the top edge of the end and center seat rails (E), no more than 1 inch (25mm) deep at the center of the rail. Narrower seat slats, about 3 inches (75mm) wide, will be needed to follow the curve.

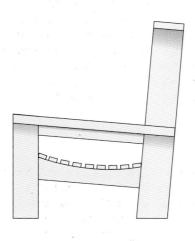

11 Carefully mark the position of the holes for screwing the seat slats to the seat rails beneath. Drill, glue and screw the slats to the seat rails. Counterbore as before to a depth of ⅜ inch (10mm) using a ½ inch (13mm) spade bit.

13 Position yourself behind the bench and, holding each slat as you go, trace the curved line of the top rail on the back of the slats. Remove the slats, cut them to the curve and reposition them against the batten and top rail. Drill, glue and screw the slats to the top rail, ensuring your drill lines follow the curve, and counterbore as usual. Nail the lower ends to the back batten.

12 Establish exactly how far back the top rail sits by measuring the distance from the rail to the front surface of the back leg. Use this measurement to position the back batten (H) on the rear seat slat. Glue and nail the batten in place. Now place the back slats in position. They should stand squarely on the rear seat slat, against the batten and the top rail. Ensure that wide and narrow slats alternate and that the spacing between slats is consistent.

14 The capping rail (K) is attached to the top rail with its front edge flush with the back slats. For it to fit cleanly, the curve of the top rail must continue to the tops of the back legs. Clamp a thin batten along the top rail and use it as a guide to carry the curve onto the top of the legs (fig.14.1). Use a square to continue the mark round the leg and cut to shape with a handsaw.

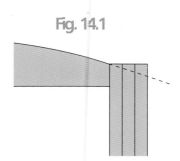

Fig. 14.1

CHANGING THE BACK

For contrast, we built the back from two alternating widths of slats, but you can adjust this according to your preference and the wood you have available. Remember that an odd number of slats looks better than an even one because the central slat will define the top of the curve. The top rail doesn't have to be curved; you could cut out shapes in the back as illustrated in other projects; or you could use narrow slats rather than alternating wide and thin boards. A further option is to make a fan back, similar to that on an Adirondack chair.

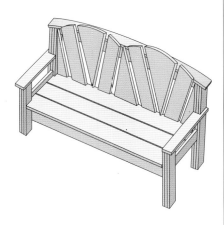

15 Drill, glue and screw the capping rail to the top back rail, working from one end to the other (fig. 15.1). The wood will curve more easily than you might imagine, but the operation is made easier if you have an assistant to help you. Counterbore the holes as usual.

Fig. 15.1

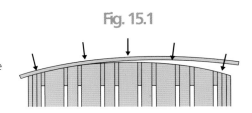

16 Mark and cut notches in the armrests (L) so they fit around the back legs. Make the notches 2¼ inches (58mm) wide and 3½ inches (90mm) deep. Measure and mark the positions for attaching the armrests to the supports, and drill, glue and screw the arm rests to the supports. Counterbore the holes as usual.

18 Glue and plug all counterbored holes with hardwood plugs. If you intend to use the plugs as a decorative feature, make sure they line up neatly at the ends of the seat slats and especially along the front edge of the seat slats. Once the glue has set, trim off any excess with a chisel to just above the surface and then sand flush. Sand all rough areas and chamfer sharp edges and corners before applying your choice of finish.

17 Place a straightedge vertically against the outside edge of the armrest to establish where to cut off the ends of the curved top rail. Trim the ends and sand smooth with a sanding block.

Wheelbarrow Bench

Being able to move a bench around the yard not only makes it easier to mow the lawn; it also allows you to follow the sun or shade throughout the day and through the seasons. Garden benches are traditionally too heavy to move. But by combining the features of a chair and a wheelbarrow, you can make a mobile bench that you can move as you wish. The plywood wheel rotates smoothly on two sealed bearings, which you should be able to obtain from any good hardware store. Alternatively, if you can't easily locate a source of sealed bearings in your area, you can recycle them from old bicycle wheels.

► This cleverly designed bench allows you to create a stylish seating area in any part of your yard.

This bench is built on a chassis-like frame, almost as if it were a vehicle. The design is simple yet sturdy, making an unusual but very versatile addition to your garden furniture.

2 Clamp the handles together and mark the positions of the cross members (B) as shown in fig. 2.1. Lay out the wheel supports (C) alongside the handles with one end of the supports flush against the cross member nearest the handles. Mark the intersection of the cross members and the wheel supports.

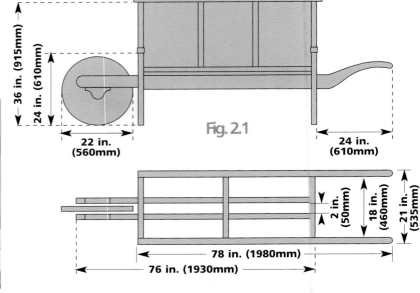

Fig. 2.1

54 in. (1370mm)

36 in. (915mm)

24 in. (610mm)

22 in. (560mm)

24 in. (610mm)

2 in. (50mm)

18 in. (460mm)

21 in. (535mm)

78 in. (1980mm)

76 in. (1930mm)

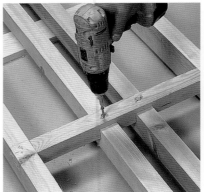

1 First construct the "chassis" to which you will attach the seat and legs. Make a plywood template for the handle sections (A) using fig 1.1 as a guide and cut the handles from 2 x 6 boards. Support the board on a pair of sawbenches and use a circular saw to cut the straight sections and a coping saw to cut the curves. Smooth the cuts with a power sander.

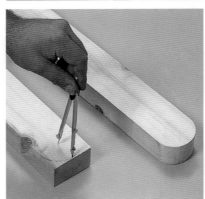

3 Use a compass to mark the curves on the ends of the wheel supports. Cut them out with a jigsaw and sand all the edges smooth; it's much easier to do this now than to wait until you've finished making the bench.

4 Measure and mark the position of the cross-halving joints in the cross members and wheel supports. The gap between the wheel supports is 2 inches (50mm). Cut the notches to a depth of 1 inch (25mm) with a tenon saw and chisel out the waste.

5 Drill, countersink and screw the handles to the cross members with two screws per side. Next, apply glue to the cross-halving joints on the cross members and wheel supports. Screw the cross members to the wheel supports. By now the chassis will be fairly rigid.

Fig. 1.1

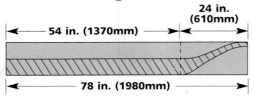

24 in. (610mm)

54 in. (1370mm)

78 in. (1980mm)

PAINTING

Make sure you paint the wheel before you assemble the piece. It's much harder to do this after the unit is finished.

ASSEMBLING SQUARE

It is important to make sure the bench is square at the critical moment when you add the armrests and the top back rail—components that will make the piece more rigid. Use a T- square to check the joints and look over all the parts to ensure the entire thing looks right.

6 Lay the front legs (D) and back legs (E) together. Mark guidelines across the legs at 12 inches (305mm) and 17½ inches (445mm) from one end. This is where they are screwed to the handles. Drill and countersink neat holes for the screws and plugs.

7 Screw and glue the front and back legs to the handles. With the bench resting on its back, draw a line on the legs slightly in from the edge on both sides and chamfer the edge with a plane. Chamfering gives the piece a more professional finish.

8 Once the legs are attached to the chassis, drill, countersink and screw the armrests (F) to the tops of the front legs. They should overhang at the front by ¾ inch (18mm). Measure 24 inches (610 mm) up the back legs and mark the point at which to attach the armrests. Drill, countersink and screw through the back leg to attach the armrests at two points.

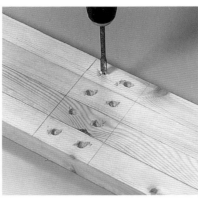

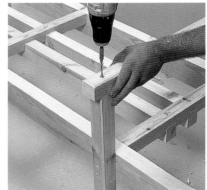

10 Position the top back rail (G) centrally on the tops of the back legs, ensuring that it overhangs both ends by equal amounts. Drill, glue and screw in place. Measure and cut lengths of batten (I) to fit round the back legs, back rail and the last of the seat slats (fig. 10.1). Glue, clamp and nail the batten in place, flush with the back edges of the bench. This batten will hold the plywood back (J) in position.

9 Glue and nail the seat slats (H) to the three cross members, working your way from front to back. Use a ½ inch (12mm) spacer to keep the gaps uniform. Make sure you position the front slat accurately as it will determine the position of the other slats. You will need to notch the back seat slat around the back leg. Mark the notch carefully before making the cut. Finally, tap the nailheads below the surface with a nail set.

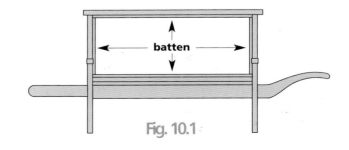

Fig. 10.1

MOLDED BACK

Rather than gluing vertical dividers to
the back, you could use moldings.
You can buy moldings at any home
store and miter them with a back saw
and miter box.

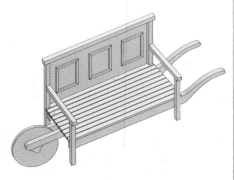

8 in. (200mm)

3½ in. (90mm)

Fig. 12.1

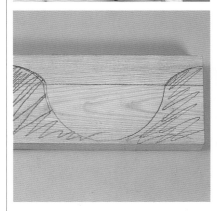

11 Glue and clamp the plywood back to the batten.
(The back can be screwed to the batten, but the
screw heads are difficult to hide if you want a natural
rather than a painted finish.) Measure and cut the back
panel dividers (K), the horizontal one to fit across the
bottom of the back between the legs, and the two
verticals between the top rail and the horizontal divider.
Glue them to the back, positioning the verticals 18 inches
(457mm) in from the inner edge of each back leg.

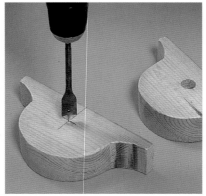

12 Mark the shapes of the axle
housings (L), using the
template shown in fig. 12.1. Use a
round object to mark the curves,
extending the line at each end. Shade
the waste area and cut out the
shapes with a jigsaw.

13 Drill the holes for the axle using
a spade bit of the same
diameter as your steel rod. The axle
must fit tightly in the hole. (Note that
the wheel actually revolves on the
bearing that is fitted in the wheel
hub.) Although this operation can be
done freehand, it's far better to use a
drill press to ensure that the holes are
drilled absolutely square to the face
of the housing.

14 Next make the wheel (M). Use
a homemade compass to mark
a circle with a diameter of 22 inches
(560mm) on the plywood. You can
either attach a piece of string to a nail
tapped into the ply and tie a pencil
11 inches (280mm) away or nail a
piece of lath or strapping to the ply
and drill a pencil hole at this distance.
Cut the wheel with a jigsaw, working
with the grain to reduce tearing.

ALTERNATIVE BACKS

For a softer look, you could make the back from vertical or horizontal slats instead of a plywood sheet. If you use horizontal slats for the back, screw them to the legs. You may need to add a central brace or support to strengthen the slats. You can make the top rail a decorative feature by cutting it longer than the others.

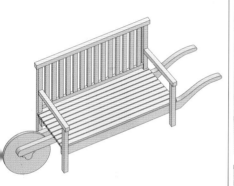

15 Drill a hole in the wheel to house the sealed bearings and axle. Start by drilling a recess around a centrally drilled pilot hole using a suitably sized flat butterfly bit. Do this on both sides of the wheel. Make sure you drill it to the correct depth for the bearing. Then use an appropriately sized drill bit to drill through the center of the wheel to accept the axle. The bearing should fit snugly in the recess and the axle should fit through the central hole. Experiment first on a piece of scrap wood to find the drill bits and drilling depth that give the best fit. Once you have drilled the central hole and the recesses, screw the bearings in place.

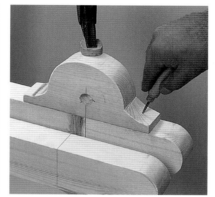

16 Fit the axle housings to the wheel supports. First drill angled pilot holes through the housing so that the screw heads will be parallel to the face. With the bench turned upside down, set the two housings in place, about two inches (50mm) from the ends of the wheel supports. Check to see they are both straight and in exact alignment with each other, clamp them in place and mark the screw locations with a bradawl.

18 Screw the axle housings to the wheel supports. Before the glue sets, test to make sure the wheel doesn't bind as it revolves. Finally, apply the finish to the bench as required.

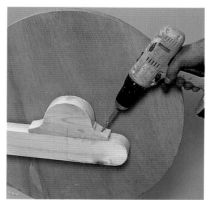
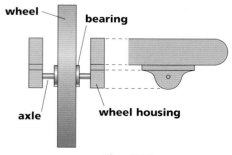

17 Before gluing, do a dry run. Assemble all the components as shown in fig 17.1 and attach the housings with screws but not glue. This allows you to determine the correct length of the axle rod. Insert the axle through the wheel, then attach the housings to each end of the rod. You may need to tap the axle into the housings with a hammer. Slot the wheel between the supports and screw the housings to them. Adjust if necessary by shortening the axle. When you are happy with the fit, re-assemble the components, adding glue this time.

wheel   **bearing**

axle   **wheel housing**

Fig. 17.1

PURPOSEFUL PLANTING: PERENNIAL VINES

FLOWERING VINES

Chinese hydrangea (*Schizophragma integrifolium*), zones 5–8

Chinese wisteria (*Wisteria sinensis*), zones 4–8

Chocolate vine (*Akebia quinata*), zones 4–8

Climbing hydrangea (*Hydrangea anomala*, spp. *Petiolaris*), zones 4–8

Climbing rose (*Rosa* cvs., 'New Dawn.' 'Dortmund'), zones 4–9

Coral plant (*Jatropha multifida*), zones 9–11

Japanese honeysuckle (*Lonicera japonica*), zones 7–9

Japanese hydrangea (*Schizophragma hydrangeoides*), zones 5–8

Japanese jasmine (*Jasminum mesnyi*), zones 8–10

Japanese wisteria (*Wisteria floribunda*), zones 5–8

Fern leaf clematis (*Clematis tangutica*), zones 4–8

Mountain clematis (*Clematis montana*), zones 4–8

Sweet pea (*Lathyrus latifolius*), zones 4–8

Trumpet vine (*Campsis radicans*), zones 5–8

Variegated weigela (*Weigela florida* 'Variegata'), zones 5–9

Winter jasmine (*Jasminum polyanthum*), zones 7–10

Mountain clematis

FOLIAGE VINES

Boston ivy (*Parthenocissus tricuspidata*), zones 4–8

Colchis ivy (*Hedera colchica*), zones 7–9

Dutchman's pipe (*Aristolochia durior*), zones 3–8

Colchis ivy

◄ *An avenue of foliage draws the eye to the trellised pagoda, which provides a secluded sanctuary in a rambling garden.*

Divisions and Doorways

Garden design these days is all about the creation of rooms—a series of interlinking outdoor spaces. Natural vegetation can separate areas of your yard, but trees, bushes, and hedges aren't always in the right places or take too long to grow. That's when you can start building your own "walls" by purchasing sections of fencing, trellis, and rail or by growing your own living fences.

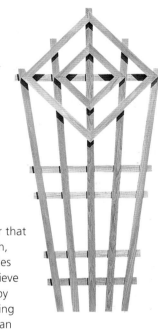

CHOOSING THE WAY YOU DIVIDE YOUR YARD

The most obvious, and certainly the quickest, way to divide a garden into rooms is to install a fence. Walls and solid fences can divide a yard into discrete zones, but they can also direct wind so it creates turbulence and drafts. Select more open divisions to absorb or filter the wind and diminish its sting, and they need less strength to resist the wind because they let some pass. You can make open divisions such as trellises from thinner, less conspicuous materials and you won't need to install substantial foundations. Of course there are also natural options: dividers that you grow or plants you train.

- Do you need to hide or protect an area instantly? Maybe you need to create boundaries to keep out strangers or provide privacy. In these cases think about solid fence panels, secured to round or square poles that are sunk into the ground. Grow plants that will climb up the fence or start a hedge just inside its boundary to hide the panels.
- Are you aiming to create areas in the yard with hidden openings? You can create doorways through divisions by overlapping lengths of hedge. The soft edges and colors of the hedge will camouflage the gap, especially if you position the hedges carefully. You can even create an archway of hedge over the entrance.

- Do you want a divider that is partially see-through, with a view of what lies beyond? You can achieve this by leaving gaps, by using sections of varying height or by creating an open structure. You can do this with trellises, wrought-iron railings or a living fence. The attraction of these options is that you can create a sense of distance and depth without diluting the impact of a specific space.
- Is maintenance an issue? Is this to be a long-lasting division or a short-term necessity? For a quick fix, you might consider installing a lightweight screen, made from decorative trellis and thin poles rather than a sturdy fence or a hedge. The screen won't require an involved installation and will also be interesting enough so you won't need to hide it with hanging plants.
- Do you want to be able to move the dividers and create a constantly evolving garden? Container plants and bushes are the ideal solution, offering mobility and longevity, although you have to be careful about where to position particular species and make sure conditions are favorable.

A Variety of Materials and Types

Most divisions and doorways in the yard are built from wood, often comprising sections of trellis, but you can also buy (or make) wrought-iron arches, railings and climbing frames. For a natural division, choose a hedge or opt for the compromise solution of a living willow fence.

WOOD

Wooden dividers work well in yards because the material blends with most environments. However the components usually have to be thicker than wrought-iron frames, so they can be more conspicuous. The beauty of wood is that it is easy to use and relatively inexpensive; pretreated wood is particularly handy. Wooden dividers are likely to look unkempt after about 10 years, but they are good value for money.

One advantage of wood is its versatility. You can use round sections for a softer look and find panels of all shapes and sizes. Trellis panels, in diamond or square patterns, break up a solid fence or can top a wall or fence to give extra protection without being visually overwhelming. Look for special connectors at the lumberyard or home store if you want to add sections of trellis to existing fences. It's also easy to create a staggered effect with trellis by simply cutting it to the dimensions you need.

When you buy wood to build a divider, you need to make sure that it is already treated with preservative or you will need to treat it yourself. If you preserve it yourself, you have the advantage of choosing the color.

▲ The pale color and tapering height of this decorative wooden pyramid help to link the cluster of deep purple bellflowers in the background with the low-growing lilac irises in the foreground.

◄ This circular gate provides a focal point in the winter landscape and in summer will host a variety of climbing plants.

◄ *The natural wood of the pergola and the green upholstery of the seat blend beautifully with red, pink and green flowers and foliage, creating a serene natural setting ideal for contemplation.*

◄► *Climbing roses enveloping an arched gateway in a picket fence (left) create a traditional and romantic setting. The white picket gate (right) is clean and light, creating a welcome invitation to explore beyond its boundary.*

WROUGHT IRON

Wrought iron is the most popular metal for creating dividers, arches and doorways. Its dimpled surface offers a softened appearance, and the traditional black finish is neutral against the many colors that fill a garden. Because it is stronger than wood, you can use thinner sections. Metal bends more easily for features such as curved arches. But be careful about mixing your materials—a wooden gate in a wrought-iron fence can look awkward.

Although wrought iron can last longer than wood, it needs more careful maintenance because it rusts quickly if the paint flakes off. You may need to rub the surface with steel wool every two or three years and apply a new coat of paint. Make sure the iron is primed with an aluminum oxide undercoat.

Wrought iron tends to be more expensive than wood and is more difficult for many gardeners to work with, although it's usually easier and less costly to install. Wrought-iron dividers tend to be climbing frames for plants, often with lengths of wire to guide and support the climbers. Consider them a long-term investment. They are likely to give a formal air to a garden, although their effect can be softened by branches, leaves and flowers growing around them.

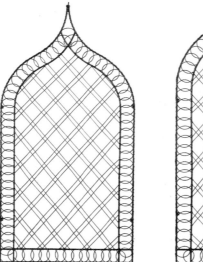

► Wrought iron is perfect for creating a sculptural impact in a garden and can be purchased in many pleasing designs.

◄ ► Vegetable gardens do not need to be purely functional. The wrought-iron arch covered with flowering clematis (left) is both beautiful and practical. Trellises such as the distinctive pyramid-shaped design (right) are ideal if you do not have room for an arch.

HEDGES

A hedge is the softest, most natural approach to dividing up a yard, but it requires regular care. If you want protection all year round, you'll probably need an evergreen hedge. Most species grow 8 feet (960mm) tall within a few years, but you must control them by pruning or they will get out of hand. Unfortunately, although you must cut them back, some of them will not grow new branches from woody areas where you've pruned.

Although many evergreens are justifiably unpopular because they grow too quickly and block light, others are softer and more manageable. For example, privet grows quickly and has little green leaves all year, while yew is very slow growing and laurel turns into a substantial hedge with large, glossy green leaves. Boxwood is used mainly for miniature hedges that punctuate paths and borders, but don't expect it to become a serious

◄ Hedges are practical, great for privacy and add structure to a yard. Privet is a popular choice for a hedge as it has foliage all year round and grows quickly.

garden divider for a generation or so. You can train and trellis fruit trees or bramble bushes to form an impenetrable hedge, but consider leaving space so you can pick from both sides. Various bamboo species can also form a good barrier.

LIVING FENCES

Living willow fences combine the qualities of hedges and fences and grow very quickly. To grow willow, insert cuttings of almost any length in to the soil during the late winter or very early spring. As long as they are

well nourished and watered, the cuttings will root and spring into life. You can weave the cuttings into a trellis design, which will thicken every year. It is up to you how tightly to weave the willow, but in wet, fertile soils, you will soon have a see-through divider that will become a more solid barrier within months. It will need lots of water, so choose its location carefully.

▲ Trained willow creates a living work of art, whether used as a fence, divider or even as a shaded seating area.

▼ ▶ The austere arch (right) in a stark environment dramatically frames the view. The heavy lines of an arched arbor (below) are softened by the profusion of sweet alyssum growing under the seat.

ARBORS, ARCHES AND TUNNELS

Arbors are a source of inspiration for many gardeners. Literally hundreds of designs, from simple arches to covered trelliswork over a bench or table, are called arbors.

Arbors can be romantic, particularly if they form a little niche where you can sit in the shade and view the garden. The ideal spot is in a corner that faces the sun so it gets lots of warmth while being protected by a "roof" of some sort. Many are positioned in the shadow of a tree, but watch out for fruit trees that might host stinging insects in the summer. An arbor can become a focal point in itself. Make it more formal with painted wooden components in Oriental or Colonial styles and plants that tightly follow the lines, or more informal with relaxed, organic shapes and a tangle of plants clinging to it.

Arches or roofed doorways can also be called arbors. Use them to form openings from one part of the garden to another, such as from the lawn to a paved area, with or without a gate. A solid gate hides what's beyond, but more open gates, such as those made from metal railings, hint at what's beyond and suggest that you're entering a special zone.

An arch might lead nowhere at all, just simply break up the monotony of a wide expanse. You can use arches to frame a special view; in that case you might want a wider arbor with a simple design so you don't interrupt the beauty of the view, but still

▲ The color of the door makes a strong statement that is echoed in the rather more subdued turquoise of the trellis arch. The small pots of pelargoniums at the foot of the door can easily be replaced with different plants when not in flower.

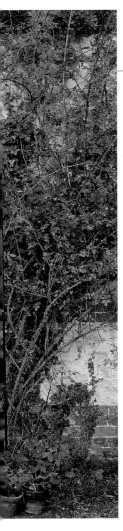

direct the eye. Japanese and Chinese styles are very popular for arches and arbors, with either very straight lines or with Lutyens-like curves and footings.

An extended arch becomes a tunnel that offers shade and the excitement of discovery. Tunnels are often used to display climbing plants because they can be seen from inside and out. They are excellent for fruiting trees and shrubs because they make picking the fruit harvest simple. You can use a tunnel as a barrier and a walkway simultaneously.

◄ *Wooden structures do not have to be rustic, as the elegant simplicity of these concentric arches demonstrates. Trailing plants soften the structure, leading the eye toward the low gate.*

► *The imposing formality and classic lines of this cast-iron gazebo are perfectly balanced by symmetrical potted shrubs, and the lines, which could be austere, are softened by trailing roses. The central urn, planted with ferns, is a subtle and understated focal point.*

PERGOLAS

Shade is a valuable commodity in the yard, and the simplest way to create it is by installing a pergola in which you can sit or dine. A pergola can be attached to a house to make a less formal and protected alternative to a sunroom or you could extend it from a sunroom to reduce the contrast between garden and home and provide a more gentle transition. Using a pergola is certainly an excellent way to unite your house and garden, while also providing shade.

The most common design is made from four or more heavy posts, joined by beams that are covered by heavy slats. With the beams and slats usually extending beyond the frame, the shadows produced by a pergola are a feature in themselves. As an extension from the house, they can even double up as a balcony if the wood is strong enough.

You can plant climbers at the base of pergolas to soften the edges, either in pots or in the ground. The latter technique needs some thought, especially if you are paving or graveling the ground below the pergola. Think about how to train the plants across the top of the pergola and use similar species to create a consistent theme. Or you may want something very leafy, like a vine, to cover the roof, but lighter, flowering plants, like clematis, to climb up the posts.

▼ *These posts, photographed on a beach, would look just as stunning in a garden setting, either as sculpture or trellis.*

TRELLIS SHAPES

Made from thin lengths of wood strips, nailed together at the joints, trellis panels are lightweight and wonderfully versatile. You can use trellis on a low wall to fill spaces upward or between the posts of a pergola.

Trellis is primarily used for training climbing plants, but that doesn't mean it can't stand unadorned. To maintain a sense of space a length of trellis with a wide square or diamond pattern allows you to see into the distance, to glimpse other parts of the garden or to blur things you don't want to see. Some people, for example, might not like looking at their vegetable patch from more formal areas. Diamond patterns are less formal than square ones.

A long length of trellis might look as solid and intimidating as fencing, so consider options for staggering

▲ ▶ *A porch created from a honeysuckle-drenched pergola provides a fragrant welcome to visitors (above). A trellis fence (right) gives a sense of space and depth to a formal garden.*

sections, with gaps you can walk through. If you use the angles cleverly, these openings can be hidden until you find them, but the trellis still breaks up the depth of view and makes it more interesting. You could also cut wider circular or square "windows" in trellis panels to accentuate a particular view and to change the focus. A row of these windows along a trellis can add formality to something that tends to be seen as a utilitarian material. The long row also provides plenty of opportunity for growing various climbing plants.

You can find sculptures made from trellis shaped like obelisks or other artistic designs. Use them on their own, with a light covering of plants, or covered and hidden by climbers. Look at color carefully because you can use pergolas to even greater effect by staining or painting them in dramatic colors.

▼ The pergola (below) blurs the lines between inside and out. Plants will seem to grow from the house.

CHOOSING THE APPROPRIATE STRUCTURE

When you need ...	Choose ...
Instant protective barrier	Solid fence panels, walls, hurdles
Long-term soft division	Trellis with climbers, hedge, living willow fence, bamboo
Blurred view into distance	Trellis, fence with openings or varied height
Structures	Trellis obelisks, sculptures, arbors, pergolas
To break up pathways	Arches, tunnels, pergolas

COMPARISON OF STRUCTURE TYPES

Characteristics	Trellis Panels	Fence Panels	Trellis Features	Pergolas	Arbors
Advantages	Lightweight and versatile; good for climbers; wind protection	Instant protection; various designs available	Wide range of designs available; easily moved	Provide shade and extra room outside; classic feature	Versatile; provide shade or frame a view; wide range of designs available
Disadvantages	Can deteriorate; needs time to give protection	Takes time to hide; wind can be funneled over fence	Can go out of fashion; not always robust	Heavy and permanent; slow to grow climbers; needs maintenance	Can go out of fashion; climbers take time to grow
Ease of Installation	Easy	Moderately easy	Very easy	Difficult	Easy to difficult, depending on the structure and design
Key Purposes	For climbers and to provide a blurred view	To hide areas and to divide two areas	As a garden feature and for climbers	To provide shade and create an outside room	Features, doorways, shady seating and to frame a view
Cost	Low	Medium	Expensive for what you get	Wood and installation can be expensive	Medium to high

◄ ▲ A large pergola (above top), adorned with a stone birdbath centerpiece, creates a seating area in the middle of a long pathway. Trellis in the shape of a gothic window (left) adds structural interest even without planting.

Tuteurs

YOU WILL NEED

FOR THE CONE

Plywood formers (A)
One 24 x 24 in. (600 x 600mm) piece
of ¾ in. (20mm) marine plywood

Legs (B)
Eight 80 in. (2000mm) 1 x 2
pressure-treated strapping

Struts (C)
Eight 40 in. (1000mm) 1 x 2
pressure-treated strapping

Hardware and finishing
Forty 1½ in. (40mm) #8 galvanized screws

FOR THE PYRAMID

Plywood formers (A)
One 20 x 20 in. (500 x 500mm) piece
of ¾ in. (20mm) marine plywood

Legs (B)
Four 80 in. (2000mm) 1 x 2
pressure-treated strapping

Long struts (C)
Four 68 in. (1700mm) 1 x 2
pressure-treated strapping

Short struts (D)
Eight 40 in. (1000mm) 1 x 2
pressure-treated strapping

Hardware and finishing
Forty 1½ in. (40mm) #8 screws

FOR THE CYLINDER

Plywood formers (A)
One 20 x 60 in. (500 x 1500mm)
¾ in. (20mm) marine plywood

Legs (B)
Four 80 in. (2000mm) 1 x 2
pressure-treated strapping

Struts (C)
Eight 72 in. (1800mm) 1 x 2
pressure-treated strapping

Hardware and finishing
Thirty-six 1½ in. (40mm) #8 screws

Tools
Basic tool kit plus large square

A tuteur, or stand-alone trellis, really comes into its own when you want a support for your favorite climbing plants. The three tuteurs here are made from plywood and strapping and are based on three simple geometric shapes—a pyramid, a cone and a cylinder.

Any of these tuteurs can be adapted to suit any size of plant. If you plan to make one much smaller than the sizes given here, use thinner strapping and plywood to prevent it from looking too bulky.

Simply push the tuteurs into the ground or stake them the same way you would stake the Hexagonal Tree Bench (page 62). If you plan to support perennials on a tuteur or leave it in the yard over the winter, make the legs longer so they can be buried to a depth below the frost line to prevent them from heaving.

► Tuteurs make eye-catching sculptural features and bring instant height to a garden. You will be able to grow a wide range of colorful climbing plants on them.

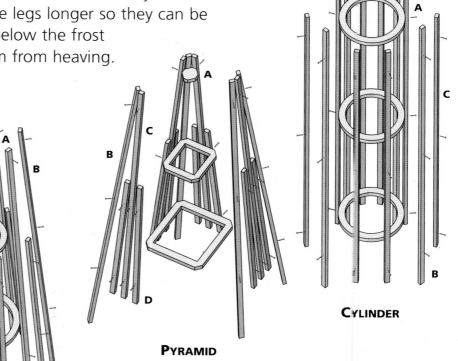

CONE

PYRAMID

CYLINDER

1 Nail one end of a batten to the center of the plywood (A). Drill holes in the batten at 7, 16 and 24 inches (175mm, 400mm and 600mm) from the nail. Put a pencil through each of the holes and draw three circles. Drill another three holes 1½–2 inches (40–50mm) inside the first three and use these to mark the inside of each circle. Cut out the circles with a jigsaw.

THE CONE

Built around concentric rings of plywood, the cone tuteur is clad in thin strapping. With judicious cutting, it's possible to cut the plywood formers from a single piece of scrap plywood. Notice how the point of the cone is truncated because the converging struts are tricky to merge.

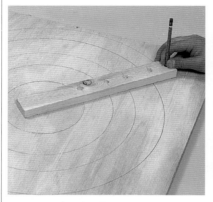

2 Cut the strapping for the legs (B) to whatever length you want, but make them all the same length. Lay them out on the floor and use a large square to mark the points where you will attach the plywood.

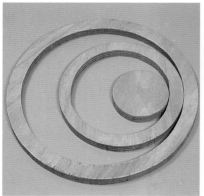

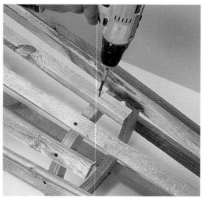

4 Space the struts (C) evenly between the legs, judging the distance by eye or by using a tape measure and drill and screw to the formers. Depending on local conditions and frost depth, the legs will need to be left between 6 and 24 inches (150–600mm) longer than the desired height so that they can be pushed deeply enough into the ground. Finish the cone with stain and wood preservative.

3 Mark the position of the legs on the formers before you assemble the cone—the legs should be spaced evenly around the circumference. The top and bottom formers should be 6 inches (150mm) from the top and the ground (not the bottom of the leg) respectively. The middle former should be halfway between the top and bottom formers. It is easiest to fix the top and bottom formers first and then to push the middle one into position and fix it where it is snug. Drill and screw the legs to the plywood formers, using a heavy post to support the structure as you work. Once you have screwed four legs onto the tuteur, it will be strong enough to stand on its own, so you can set it upright to attach the remaining legs.

1 On an offcut of plywood, mark three squares with sides of 20 inches (500mm), 13 inches (325mm) and 5 inches (125mm). The top former is solid and the lower pieces are cut to form bands 1½–2 inches (40–50mm) wide. Drill access holes and cut out the squares with a jigsaw or scrollsaw.

THE PYRAMID

As with the cone, the formers for the pyramid tuteur can be cut from a single plywood offcut. This tuteur has four legs, one on each corner, and each side is clad with one long and two short struts. You can alter the cladding to create whatever design you like.

2 Cut off the corners of the plywood squares to leave a flattened edge approximately 1½ inches wide. Support the formers with a heavy piece of wood, or even a log, then drill and screw the legs to the cut-off corners of the plywood (see Cone, step 3).

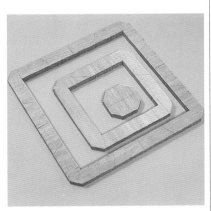

3 Place the long struts (C) on the formers, positioned centrally between the legs. Drill and screw them to all three formers. Note that the long struts stop short of flush with the legs at the top.

4 The struts are screwed to the plywood so that they will be flush with the ground once you've set up the tuteur. You can countersink the holes, but the screw heads tend to pull themselves below the surface of the strapping, giving a neater finish.

5 Position the short struts (D) between the legs and the long struts. Drill and screw them to the middle and lower formers only. Finish the pyramid with stain and clear preservative or apply ready-colored preservative.

1 To mark the circles for cutting out a formers (A), make a compass as directed for the Cone (step 1, page 111). Measure and drill two holes in the compass that will enable you to draw a ring with a diameter of 20 inches (500mm) and a width of 1½–2 inches (40–50mm).

THE CYLINDER

You need more plywood to make the formers for the cylinder tuteur than for the other designs because the rings do not fit inside each other. The construction is simple, with just four legs and eight struts of equal length, but take care when marking the location of the struts on the formers to make sure they are evenly spaced.

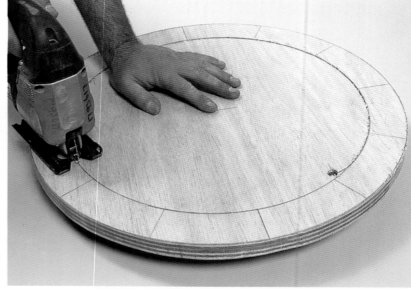

2 Drill an access hole in the plywood and cut out the formers using a jigsaw. Mark and cut out the remaining two formers in the same way.

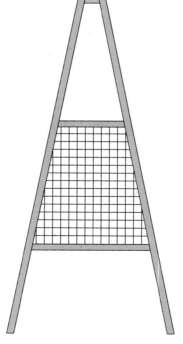

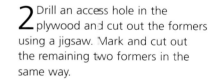

ALTERNATIVE DECORATION

You don't have to rely on strapping for decorating the tuteurs. You could attach wooden legs to the formers and fill the spaces between them with netting or wires, or fill just some of the spaces and leave others open

3 Mark the legs (B) where you intend to attach the formers. Drill the pilot holes (see Cone, step 3).

4 Use a pole or post to support the formers while you attach the legs. Space the legs evenly around the formers and check the positions of the formers on pairs of opposite legs, judging distances by eye or with a tape measure. Once you have attached the legs you can, if you prefer, stand the structure upright to attach the struts.

5 Screw the struts (C) to the formers, making sure they are evenly spaced. Any inconsistencies in the spacing will be especially apparent in the cylinder tuteur since it is defined by its straight sides. Make sure you align the struts with the tops of the legs. Finish by applying stain and either colored or clear preservative.

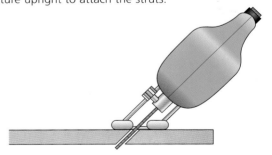

ANGLED PLYWOOD FORMERS FOR A STRONGER FIT
We've tried to keep the construction for these tuteurs really simple, but the cone and pyramid designs will be stronger if you cut the edges of the plywood formers at an angle. The best way to do this is to angle your jigsaw for the cuts around the outside edges. This will make the legs and struts sit more solidly on the formers.

Trellis Panels

Standardized trellis panels are available in every garden center and home store, but what happens if you want one in a non-standard size or shape? Fortunately, trellis panels are quick and easy to make. The only tricks are planning the shape you want and laying it out on thin plywood. During construction, the trellis will be unstable and difficult to nail together. But the more joints you nail, the more rigid the panel becomes. Here we've used a sandwich of lathing strips to give the panels added strength and a more interesting appearance than the commercial versions. This gives plenty of latitude for adjusting the size of the spaces between the lathing or creating windows or doorways in the panels.

► *Trellis panels are an easy way to make screens, dividers and archways, and provide a valuable surface for climbers, adding a splash of color to your yard.*

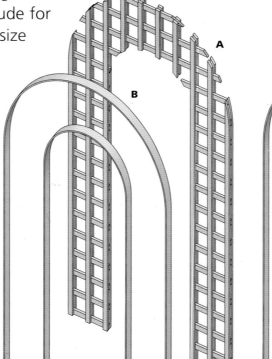

ARCHED TRELLIS

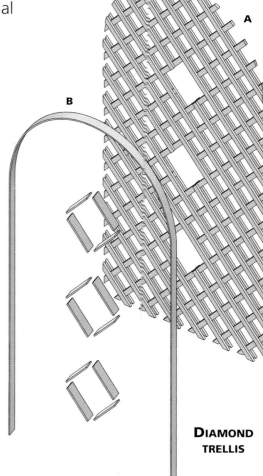

DIAMOND TRELLIS

1 Transfer the template in fig. 1.1 to the plywood sheet. To draw the curves, use a compass made from a piece of lath nailed on the centerline and 24 inches (610mm) from the top of the sheet. Drill pencil holes in the lath at 10¾, 12, 22¾ and 24 inches (275mm, 305mm, 580mm and 610mm) from the nail. Mark the

2 You now have three templates, A, B and C. Lay templates A and C on the floor and place four vertical laths on them, one at the inside and outside of each side of the arch. Trim the four central laths to size. They descend only to the top of the arch. Roughly lay all the horizontal laths on top of the verticals, again trimming them to size so as not to encroach into the arch. Line up the bottom horizontals with the bottom edge of the templates and use 4 inch (100mm) spacers to adjust for even spacing from bottom to top. Make sure the verticals are straight, then nail through all three layers to fix them together. Repeat until you've nailed all the verticals to the horizontals.

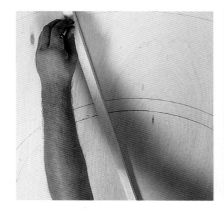

3 Position the two vertical pieces that go in the center of each side of the arch. Place one below and one above the horizontal pieces and nail through all three layers to fix them together.

curves and cut around the three outer ones with a jigsaw. Use a handsaw for the straight cuts. Do not cut the innermost curve—it is a guideline only.

Fig. 1.1

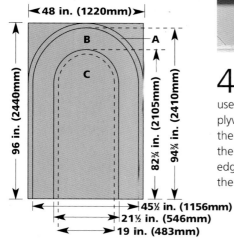

4 As the template is inaccessible since it is now under the trellis, use the curve on the outer piece of plywood scrap from which you cut the template to mark where to trim the top curve of the arch. The inner edge of the scrap corresponds with the outer edge of the template.

5 Use the compass to mark the curve of the arch on the trellis pieces. Position it in the same hole that you used to mark the template. The original mark on the template is there to show where to position the pieces for the arch; any excess can be cut off with a jigsaw once you've assembled the trellis.

6 Nail lengths of plywood lining strip all the way around the inside edge of the trellis. Repeat this process for the outside edge, then apply your chosen finish. To erect the arch in the yard, dig a hole about 12 inches (300mm) deep for each side, insert the arch and replace the soil, firming it around the base on each side.

YOU WILL NEED

FOR THE TRELLIS

Template
One 24 x 48 in. (1220 x 2440mm) sheet
of ⅛ in. (3mm) marine plywood

Trellis (A)
Twenty-eight 80 in. (2m) lengths of
1¼ x ½ in. (30 x 13mm) lathing

Lining (B)
Six strips of ⅛ in. (3mm) marine plywood
measuring 72 in. (1.8m) long by 1½ in.
(38mm) wide

Hardware and finishing
Two hundred and fifty 1¼ in. (30mm)
galvanized finish nails

Wood preservative, paint, stain, varnish

Tools
Basic tool kit

EXPERIMENTING WITH SHAPES

Experiment with different shapes by
adjusting the angles of the lathing
strips and by altering the shape of
the top. You can have a straight top,
a pointed top or a top with a
shallower or steeper curve.

◄ 48 in. (1220mm) ►

96 in. (2440mm)

94¾ in. (2410mm)

45½ in. (1156mm)

Fig. 1.1

1 Transfer the template in fig. 1.1 to the plywood sheet. Make a compass
from a piece of lath nailed in the center of the rectangle and 24 inches
(610mm) from the top. Drill pencil holes in the lath at 22¾ and 24 inches
(580mm and 610mm) from the nail. Draw the curves and cut both outer and
inner shapes with a jigsaw. Set a combination square to 45 degrees and mark
guidelines on the outer template to define the angle of the lathing strips. You
will use the template to size and cut all the laths that form the trellis screen.
Cut the pieces overlong so you can trim them flush with the edge of the
template at a later stage.

2 Take a short trellis piece and
position it on a 45 degree
guideline on either of the bottom
corners of the template. Roughly lay
out the pieces for all three layers of
the trellis sandwich. Starting in one of
the bottom corners, begin nailing the
layers together, checking to see the
pieces are square to one another. Use
4 inch (100mm) spacers to position
the next row, nail that in place and
move on.

4 Once the trellis is assembled, cut
out three diamond-shaped
windows down the center by simply
sawing off the diagonal crossing laths
at one-square intervals, starting no
lower than 24 inches (600mm) from
the bottom of the trellis. Line the
windows with the plywood lining
strip before applying the finish of
your choice. Erect the trellis panel as
described on page 118.

3 Once you have nailed all the pieces
together, cut off the ends at a 45 degree
angle so they are flush with the edges of
the inner template. Then use the outer
template to mark the curve at the top of
the trellis. Raise the panel off the ground on
blocks and cut the curve with a jigsaw. Nail
a plywood lining strip all the way around
the sides and top of the panel, attaching
the nails to the two outer trellis pieces or
the single inner piece as appropriate.

Arbor

YOU WILL NEED

Posts (A)
Four 108 in. (2700mm) 4 x 4 pressure-treated softwood fence posts

Bottom cross members (B)
Two 36 in. (900mm) 2 x 4 pressure-treated sawn softwood

Top cross members (C)
Two 56 in. (1400mm) 2 x 4 pressure-treated roughsawn softwood

Vertical trellis fixings (D)
Four 72 in. (2000mm) 1 x 2 pressure-treated strapping

Horizontal trellis fixings (E)
Four 36 in. (1000mm) 1 x 2 pressure-treated strapping

Trellis panels (F)
Two 72 x 36 in. (1800 x 900mm) trellis panels

Roofing joists (G)
Four 48 in. (1200mm) 2 x 4 pressure-treated sawn softwood

Roof strappings (H)
Four 56 in. (1400mm) 1 x 4 pressure-treated sawn softwood

Ridge (I)
One 68 in. (1700mm) 1 x 6 pressure-treated sawn softwood

Hardware and finishing

Thirty-two 3 in. (75mm) #10 galvanized screws for main structural members

Forty 1½ in. (35mm) #8 galvanized screws for trellis and supports

Wood preservative, paint, stain, varnish

Polyethylene sheeting (if concreting posts into ground)

Four twin-bolt 4 in. (100mm) post supports (if bolting the posts to concrete slab)

Tools

Basic tool kit plus mallet and marking gauge

Note: This project makes use of sawn lumber, which has a rougher finish than milled or square-edged wood, but is considerably cheaper.

I n smaller gardens, where trees are few and far between, an arbor offers shade and support—without taking up too much space. Climbing plants can scale the sides and cascade over the roof, providing a semi-natural division or doorway. Add a seat and a back support and you've created a private retreat!

This is garden carpentry at its simplest and a great introduction to building structures. The posts are set into the ground, with or without concrete, using ready-made trellis as panels on the sides. We've chosen to make a pitched roof, but it could just as easily be curved or even an Oriental design. Since the sides are self-supporting, you could alter the top later if your tastes change.

There are two ways to make this type of structure. You can gather all the parts at hand, then sink the posts into the ground and join them with panels. This way, assembling the parts will be easier if you are working alone. Alternatively, you can construct the panels, dig the holes, and sink the posts with the panels already attached. You will need more people to handle the panels, but the pieces are sure to fit and you'll do less adjusting on site. We've chosen the latter course.

▶ *This arbor makes a handsome focal point at the end of a lawn, or position it more discreetly in a border or a wooded area to create a retreat.*

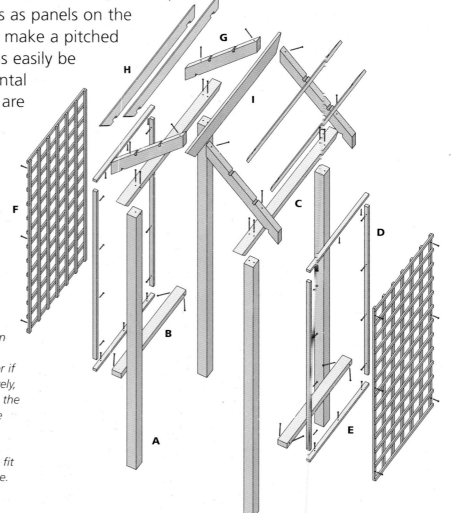

2 Ensure the bottom cross member (B) is the right length for your trellis panel (F). Drill a hole at a low angle at the ends of the bottom cross member and screw it to the posts with one screw from each side.

3 Mark the ends of the top cross member (C) at 45 degrees using a protractor, then mark across the width using a combination square. Cut the ends off with a handsaw.

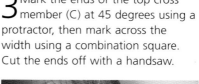

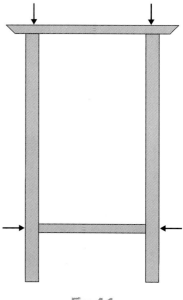

Fig. 4.1

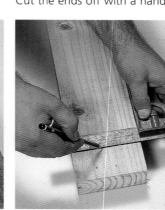

1 Take two of the posts (A) and mark the positions for the bottom cross member (B), 6½ inches (165mm) above ground level. Make sure the positions are identical on both posts. (Remember to leave plenty of post below the trellis for sinking into the ground. The hole in the ground should be about one third to one quarter of the height of the structure. (We recommend leaving 28 inches [700mm] on the end of each post if you are sinking it into concrete.) Mark the positions for the bottom cross member on the other two posts.

4 Position the posts and top cross member at right angles to each other and screw the top cross member in place with two screws (fig. 4.1). The top cross member should overhang by about 6 inches (150mm) at each end. The assembly won't be that secure yet, so leave it on a flat piece of ground.

5 Mark the position of the trellis fixings (D and E) that will attach the trellis to the posts and cross members, remembering to place the fixings on the inside so that they are hidden from view most of the time.

6 Drill and screw the trellis fixings to the posts and top and bottom cross members. They should be 1 inch (25mm) in from both sides of the post. Make sure they all line up.

ORNAMENTAL ENDS

Rather than simply cutting angled ends to the roof strappings, you could cut more ornamental curves and shapes, using a jigsaw.

ADDING A SEAT

It's very simple to add a slatted seat to the arbor. Simply screw cross members slightly higher, about 16 inches (400mm) above the ground, and attach slats for a seat. You'd probably want to add a trellis panel to the back and can choose whether or not to have trellis below the seat on either side.

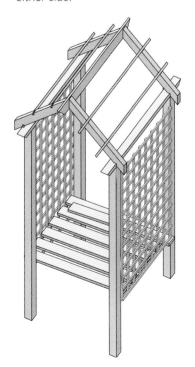

7 Screw the trellis panel (F) to the trellis fixings. This will strengthen the assembly considerably and it can now be moved around safely. Assemble the other side of the arbor in exactly the same way.

9 Use the drawing to mark one of the roofing joists, to calculate the angle for the pitch and to mark the positions for the roof strappings (H) (fig. 9.1).

8 If you haven't built a roof before, it's well worth drawing the roof shape out full size on a piece of plywood. This helps you to work out the pitch and the angles you need to cut. Here we've gone for a 40 degree roof pitch, but you could adjust this to suit your tastes.

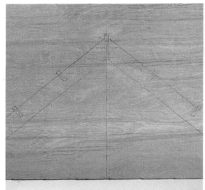

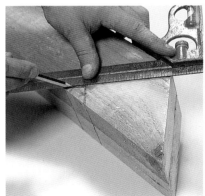

10 Cut the ends of the joists and clamp them in pairs. Mark the positions of the bird's-mouth notches, which will locate the joists on the upper cross members. They are cut at 40 degrees to the sides of the roofing joists and at a depth and height of $1\frac{3}{16}$ x $1\frac{3}{16}$ inches (30 x 30mm).

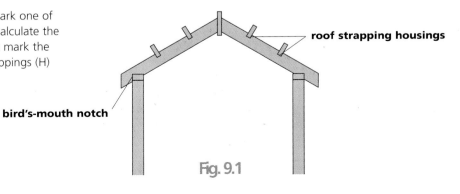

roof strapping housings

bird's-mouth notch

Fig. 9.1

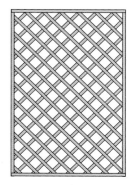

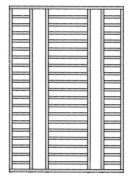

TRELLIS OPTIONS

Use wire or mesh instead of filling the sides of the arbor with trellis. Buy different styles of trellis or make your own. Diamond pattern is an obvious choice, but you could also use a series of thin trellis panels, rather than one per side.

11 Cut the housings for the roof strappings to a depth of 1 inch (25mm). Measure the positions of the housings and the notch from the ridge end of the roofing joist. The first housing should be 13½ inches (343mm) from the end; the second 27¾ inches (705mm). The vertical cut for the bird's-mouth notch should be 36⅝ inches (930mm) from the end.

12 Clamp the four roof strappings (H) and mark the notches in one operation to position them accurately. Cut the notches to a depth of 1 inch (25mm). Use a protractor to mark a 45 degree angle on the end of the strappings to match the angle at the end of the top cross members. Cut with a handsaw.

13 The roofing strappings and joists should now slot together neatly. You can assemble each side of the roof with the strappings and joists to see how it all fits together. Use a protractor to mark a 45 degree angle on either end of the the ridge and cut with a handsaw.

14 Mark the positions of the roofing joists on the ridge: they should be 38 inches (965mm) apart and 25 inches (635mm) from each end. Assemble the roof by screwing the joists to the ridge, then strengthen them by fitting the strappings in place. Nail a temporary batten across the joist ends to stop the roof from spreading while you fix the assembly to the top cross member.

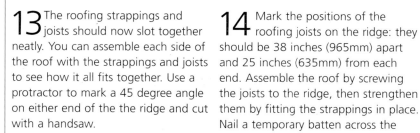

ALTERNATIVE ROOFS

Instead of the pitched roof, you could create an arch, but you would need to use plywood for the joists. In that case you might prefer to paint the arbor, though stain and varnish could also work. Alternatively you could make a simple Japanese-style arbor with horizontal roof joists that are very slightly curved.

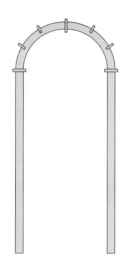

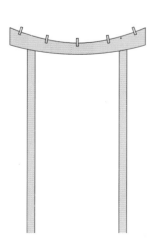

15 Excavate four holes in the ground about 28 inches (700mm) deep and 12 inches (300mm) wide, with their centers matching the post positions. The posts can be set into holes with concrete or clamped into post supports that are then bolted to a concrete slab set into the ground. If you are using a concrete slab, we recommend that it be 12 x 12 inches (300 x 300mm) in size and 1½ to 2 inches (40 to 50mm) thick. If you intend to set the posts in concrete, wrap the ends in polyethylene to stop them from rotting. Position the arbor in the holes, one side at a time, and fill each hole with concrete, about two-thirds full. Temporarily brace the arbor side while you position the other side (see the Child's Fort project, page 152, for more tips on concreting posts).

16 For stability while you continue construction, brace the roof section together temporarily with battens to match the measurements of the vertically set posts. The roofing joists can then be drilled and screwed to the ridge, using one screw per joist.

17 Drill and screw the roof strapping to the joists. Just before you raise the assembled roof onto the arbor, remove the temporary battens.

18 Get a friend to help you lift the roof onto the arbor and to locate the bird's-mouth notches on the top cross members. When you are happy with the position drill and screw the joists to the top cross members. Finally, apply the wood preservative, stain or varnish of your choice.

PURPOSEFUL FEEDING

THE RIGHT SEED FOR THE JOB

▶ Black oil sunflower seed is easier for all birds to crack, but some favor shelled seed as hearts, chips, or kernels.

◀ Mixes combine various seeds to suit different birds. Safflower is a common ingredient.

▶ Nyjer is a new small black seed that's good for small birds like goldfinches and pine siskins.

HOME-MADE FOOD

- Robins will eat cheese.
- Blackbirds, thrushes and redwings like apples.
- Siskins, greenfinches and woodpeckers eat unsalted, raw peanuts. Juncos and sparrows like shelled nuts.
- Orioles are attracted by orange halves and grape jelly.
- Woodpeckers, nuthatches and wrens like suet, hung from a tree in a wire holder.
- Hang banana skins near nectar feeders to attract fruitflies for hummingbirds.
- Pour salty water over a log to form crystals, which grosbeaks and redpolls eat.
- Make your own bars from various combinations of suet, bird seed, peanut butter and flour or meal. See which birds eat them.

TOP TIPS FOR HEALTHIER BIRDS

- Move bird feeders every year.
- Clear away stale or soggy food.
- Don't overfeed.

◀ This ingenious construction provides much-needed shade for amphibians as well as functioning as an attractive pond feature.

Wildlife Winners

Wildlife brings a yard to life, with birdsong and animal movement adding an essential dimension to the garden. Homes for birds and animals can be used as features or simply to encourage wildlife, and are available in all manner of styles for various species. Look after your wildlife and you'll have a vibrant yard.

Whether it's to spark a child's curiosity or for company as you garden or lounge, the sound and sight of birds, insects and small animals is a valuable asset to the yard. With urban wildlife, provision of food and protection can help threatened species survive. Birds are the most obvious form of wildlife to attract. You can easily build your own feeding stations, birdhouses and nesting boxes and be rewarded by feathered friends that return year after year.

▼ It is important that you fill bird feeders such as this hopper with seed that is suitable for the local bird population, especially if you wish to attract a particular species to your garden.

CHOOSING YOUR WILDLIFE WINNERS

The most dangerous animal in the zoo, say some keepers, is man. If you want to bring wildlife to your yard, it is important to decide which animals you want to attract and provide suitable feed and habitat.

- Do you want birds to nest near your home? Look at the various options for birdhouses and dovecotes, making sure you position them where predators will find it difficult to steal eggs or chicks.
- Is it important for you to attract particular breeds of bird? Hummingbirds, for instance, like nectar and you can buy special feeders. Local pet stores can tell you what feed to use to attract specific breeds.
- Do you want to help all sorts of wildlife? You can provide homes for insects and small mammals by creating the appropriate habitat, and this can help the local food chain, although such habitats may also attract animals you do not want.
- Do you want to keep some predators out? You may need to consider fencing off some areas of the yard to protect plants and vegetables from certain animals. Think about clearing undergrowth or piles of rotting wood if you want to keep out unwanted spiders or snakes.

Feeders, Boxes and Baths

Because they are so colorful and active, birds are the most popular of animals to attract. Feeding devices and nesting boxes are easy to buy or build, but they may need protection from predators, especially if you are also helping to support squirrels, foxes and other small animals in your yard.

PROTECTING WILDLIFE

One of the great myths of our time is that you should feed birds only in the winter. What people often forget is that during spring and early summer, food may still be scarce, just when birds and animals are feeding their young. The food and housing you supply depends on the species you want to attract, and those you'd prefer to deter.

Squirrels, for instance, are very playful characters that many people admire for their agility and hoarding instincts. Others consider squirrels vermin, and they will go to any lengths to keep their yards free of the bushy-tailed beasts. One solution is to give squirrels their own food and entertainment, with special swings, munch boxes, tables, twirling wheels for corn and other feeders to distract them from bird feeders.

Domestic cats have become the most common menace to birds, especially in cities. In some parts of the world, they are responsible for dramatic declines in certain bird species. Fortunately you can protect the birds you invite. Baffles above hanging bird feeders and below raised models can inhibit both cats and squirrels. A block of wood, set outside the hole of a nest box, stops these animals from reaching inside to attack chicks. Perches for birds give them time to check for predators before they settle to feed.

▲ Bat populations are in decline, but by providing homes such as this bat house, you can help to protect them as well as bring a fantastic method of natural pest control into your garden.

You may want to attract bats by providing shelter, although birds may choose to inhabit unused bat boxes. Bats suffer when gardens are cleaned up since they like rotten logs and trunks.

YOUR OWN WILDLIFE CENTER

Wherever you live, you always have the potential to transform your backyard into a wildlife center. You may have ambitious plans for creating attractive environments for insects, reptiles, animals and birds, but take some caution. A pile of logs covered with dead leaves and twigs is the ideal home for snakes in some climates and may tempt more troublesome visitors.

One of the simplest ways to draw wildlife to your garden is not to clean it up too much. Dead trees are nesting and perching sites for

▲ This feeder has a grille to protect the birds' food from squirrels. The feeder is mounted on a pole but also has a ring on the roof to allow it to be suspended.

many birds, and they act as homes for many insects and small animals, which birds appreciate as food. Birds will thank you for not deadheading all the flowers, since they enjoy the ripened seed.

Foxes like living under sheds, which is one good reason for raising such buildings above the ground a little, rather than laying a concrete base. Bees will nest in clay pots sunk below the ground, with only the hole in the base showing, especially if you stuff rodent bedding into the pot. Create a shallow pond with a liner in a shady spot for frogs, toads and other damp-loving amphibians, reptiles and insects.

▲ ▼ *It is best to use a squirrel feeder (above) if you want squirrels in your yard without disrupting the bird life. Lend nesting birds a helping hand by providing soft material for them to pluck out and add to their nest (below).*

▼ ▶ *Traditional dovecotes (at right) make a beautiful garden feature, as well as providing a home for these lovely creatures. This elegant copper bird feeder (below) is stylish as well as practical. The conical roof serves as a weather baffle to protect the seed from inclement weather, while the base provides a good perch.*

WHAT'S AVAILABLE

Garden centers are crammed with products for feeding and protecting birds. Most birdboxes and feeding stations are made from plastic or wood and differ in style and design to suit the size and species of birds as well as the circumstances of your yard and home. Some of the less expensive options may be fine outside your kitchen door but look too crude hanging from a decorative tree in the garden. There are also systems for attaching feeders to railings around a balcony.

Make sure you provide the right environment for your local wildlife, taking precautions to protect birds from predators. Many birds want hedges, trees and bushes for nesting, although others favor building their nests under the eaves or inside outbuildings and barns. To make sure the habitat suits local birds, talk to someone knowledgeable about the wildlife in your area, such as a landscaper or someone from an animal protection agency.

It is important to buy or build the right nesting boxes and feeders for

the birds in your area. Check with local experts and follow our guidelines for purposeful feeding (page 127). Don't forget that birds also need water to bathe and drink as well as shelter and food.

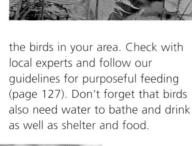

◀ This classic birdhouse design provides both a sheltered nesting place and good protection from predators such as neighborhood cats.

◀ ▼ Birdbaths are available in many different designs, from an iron pedestal adorned with a bird (at left) to a combined birdbath and sundial (below). Whatever the design, the most important thing is that it is high enough above the ground to offer protection from predators.

▼ The classic bird table is just that—a platform on which to put food. This example has the added advantage of a roof to keep the food—and the birds—dry.

BIRD FEEDERS

The simplest bird table is exactly that: an aircraft carrier where birds can land to nibble sprinkled tidbits and drink from a saucer of water. A roof protects the diners, ensuring their food doesn't get ruined by rain, frost or sunshine. Bread is, reportedly, bad for birds' health, but plenty of people swear by scattering the crumbs of burnt toast on the most basic of bird tables, with a few other seeds and leftovers. The fanciest bird tables have thatched roofs and are made from thin "logs" or split logs for a softer look.

These days, however, you can get special feeding systems to match the types of food your local birds enjoy. A hopper works well for the larger seeds like sunflower and safflower and is usually designed as a rectangular structure with a sloping roof. Holes around the base allow seed to filter down on demand. A tray underneath catches any dropped food. The roof acts as a lid for refilling, and the sides are sometimes transparent to show the level and condition of the food, which should be checked regularly for dampness.

Some birds prefer the simplicity of a hopper. According to the U.S. National Bird-Feeding Society, cardinals, jays, sparrows, nuthatches and some finches prefer hoppers, but they are not suitable for smaller seeds like black Nyjer or sunflower chips.

The alternative is to hang a tubular feeder from a tree or pole. Most people have used a sock or net of food for birds, but there are more sturdy models with perches and reinforced feeding holes plus a tray and a roof. Some birds will sit on the perch to eat; others will take their meal home. Goldfinches prefer to peck upside down, with the perch above the hole. The most complicated designs have a protective wire skirt around the outside, to keep large birds and animals out. Choose or cut holes to suit the type of food you intend to dispense and put cat litter in the bottom of the tube feeder to soak up moisture.

To attract birds close to the house, add a window feeder to your portfolio of devices. Place it on the windowsill or attach it to the glass with suction cups so you can view the birds from the warmth of your home as they feed. Some of these use mirrors to screen you from skittish creatures.

◄ Hanging bird feeders are clean, practical and more versatile than traditional bird tables.

◄ Window-mounted bird feeders can bring a little bit of nature into your home even if you live in an apartment.

▲ The elongated wire mesh sides on this feeder allow a number of birds to cling to the sides at any one time.

◄ ► Hummingbird feeders (left) do not require perches because the birds hover when drinking. The woodpecker feeder (right) has a metal grille for the bird to grip and peck through to reach the food.

NEST BOXES

Birds that breed in your yard are more likely to feed from your hoppers, tubes and tables. And with a few skills you can build a simple bird house from ¾ inch (18mm) thick wood in no time. Make one hole for access and smaller ones in the sides and bottom for light, ventilation, and drainage. Some species, like flycatchers and robins, need little more than a simple tray or platform fitted to a wall, with a roof just for cover and they'll start building a nest. Others don't even need the roof.

The trouble is that birds are pickier than you might imagine. The hole mustn't be too small or too large and must be positioned just right, usually without a landing platform but with a step-up inside. However nice you make the box look, it's the size and shape of the interior that birds judge during the weeks and months from January on that they spend searching for a home. Some prefer to nest high, others only a few feet off the ground.

Wood is the best material for building nest boxes. It is one of the more attractive materials for gardens, offers good insulation in winter and summer and can also be pecked and altered. Use untreated timber, which provides good camouflage, only reinforcing it with metal to protect it from woodpeckers if they are a problem.

A good way to start is to buy a kit for a specific species; it will come with instructions on positioning. Walls are better places to locate a box or tray than trees, which provide predators with easy access. Try to keep the box out of direct sunlight and to select a spot that offers the natural protection of climbers or vines. Birds are territorial, so you're most likely to have success by targeting a range of species, providing them with the facilities where and when they expect. A little research will soon confirm what you need to supply for your local bird population.

▶ *If you want to place a nest box in a tree, suspend the box from a suitable branch to avoid the risk of climbing predators gaining access to it.*

▶ *Round apertures allow access to small birds, while butterflies enter through long, narrow slits (right). A wooden house is the most common design of nest box (far right).*

BIRDBATHS

Birds need water to quench thirst and to keep clean, but it also helps them digest food. The best bath is relatively shallow, never deeper than 2 inches (50mm) at the center, and can be made either from decorative stone or an upturned garbage can lid. It needs to be regularly refilled or changed because the water gets dirty quickly and can pass diseases between birds. Diluted bleach gets rid of algae, but must be rinsed away after cleaning, and vinegar clears lime deposits.

Positioning the birdbath is critical. Wet birds are at their most vulnerable from predators. Baths need to be raised at least 3 feet (900mm) off the ground to deter cats and are best sited near a tree or bush so birds can escape. In fact, a bath suspended from a tree also gives cover to birds threatened by hawks. The tinkle of water from a dripper or fountain will attract more visitors. Hummingbirds, in particular, like to fly through a watery mist. Some birds, like titmice, chickadees and goldfinches, will actually drink from the dripper.

In the depths of winter, water can become a precious commodity for birds who may be able to "drink" snow, but cannot break ice. You can buy birdbaths with built-in coils to keep the water warm, and some are even solar-powered. A cover over the bath reduces the risk of freezing.

▼ *A bath with a fluted edge and a pair of lovebirds makes a pretty but practical addition to a romantic garden design.*

▼ ► *The copper construction (right) gives a contemporary twist to the traditional birdbath. A stone birdbath set in a flower garden is attractive to both birds and humans (below).*

COMPARISON OF BIRD-FEEDING DEVICES

Device	Feeding Table	Hopper	Tube Feeder
Versatility	Good	Medium	Low to medium
Durability	Tends to wear quickly without roof	Plastic panels can cloud quickly	Many have lifetime guarantee from squirrel damage, though cheap versions break easily
Beauty	Can be decorative, but often functional	More functional than beautiful, though more decorative versions can be made from wood	Lovely display of acrobatic birds, but not very attractive
Materials	Ideally round wood pole; roof shingles, thatch or wood	Usually plastic or metal, but also wood	Largely plastic and wire
Advantages	Can be used for any food; can hang other feeders from the table	Takes large quantity of food and keeps it dry; wooden ones look good	Inexpensive and wide range of options available; models with built-in baffle readily available
Disadvantages	Takes a battering; needs to be resited every year; must have a baffle	Limited to larger seed, which tends also to get scattered and spilled; must have a baffle; more expensive than other tables and tubes	Usually in plastic; doesn't carry much food; doesn't always suit garden environment
Cost	Low to medium	Medium to high	Low to medium

Birdfeeder

This distinctive chalet-style birdfeeder features a mock cedar-shingle roof that you create by cutting shallow kerfs or grooves into strips of thin plywood. There's a hole for a food container. Attach the whole thing to a wall or mount it on a pole as shown. The gable ends are finished with decorative bargeboards, made by drilling a series of holes into a board and then sawing along the length to cut the holes in half. Skip this step to save time, but the trim will give the birdfeeder a longer life and adds a lot to its attractiveness.

▶ *Beautifully proportioned and rich in architectural detail, the birdfeeder will attract even the most discerning of species.*

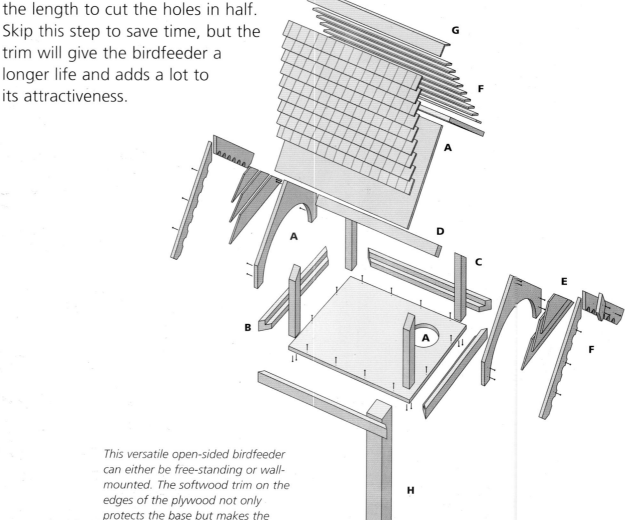

This versatile open-sided birdfeeder can either be free-standing or wall-mounted. The softwood trim on the edges of the plywood not only protects the base but makes the birdfeeder look more substantial.

1 Cut the pieces for the base, gables and roof (A) out of the plywood, following the plan and measurements in fig. 1.1. Mark the curves with a compass and use a handsaw and a jigsaw to cut the different shapes. Then cut the pieces of molding for the base trim (B), using the base as a guide to determine the lengths of the pieces. Miter the ends for a neat fit.

2 Mark and cut a hole for a plastic container that will hold bird food. Ideally, the container should have a rim or be tapered so that it can just drop into the hole.

3 Glue and nail the softwood molding pieces to the plywood base. If you are unable to locate suitable molding, use a router or hand plane to cut a rabbet in a piece of 2 x 2 softwood to fit.

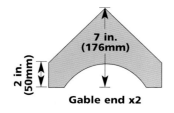

7 in. (176mm)

2 in. (50mm)

Gable end x2

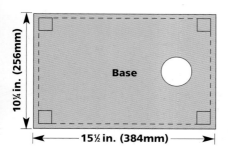

10¼ in. (256mm)

Base

15½ in. (384mm)

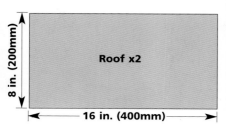

8 in. (200mm)

Roof x2

16 in. (400mm)

Fig. 1.1

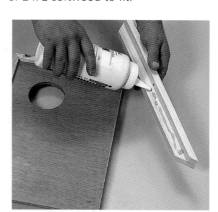

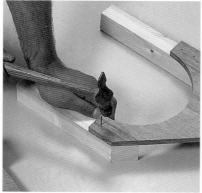

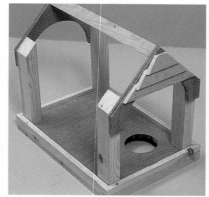

4 You can now start constructing the walls and roof. Use the arched gable ends (A) to mark the angles at the tops of the softwood pillars (C) and cut to shape. Attach the pillars to the base by nailing up through the bottom of the base. Nail the ridge pole (D) between the gable ends.

5 With the basic structure in place, cut out and attach the cladding (E) to the gables. Start with the bottom strip and work your way up, using the gables to measure the length and mark the angles of each piece to cut. Nail the pieces in place, allowing them to overlap slightly and making sure each strip is parallel with the adjacent piece.

6 Attach the plywood roof (A) to the end frames. You can do this with glue; it doesn't need to be nailed in place.

MOUNTING THE FEEDER

To mount the birdfeeder on a pole, attach blocks to the underside of the base to make a mortise where you can insert the pole. Take care that the blocks don't interfere with the hole for the food container. Secure the pole in the ground using one of the methods described on page 125.

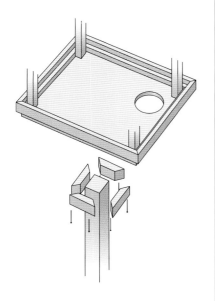

7 Next make the roof shingles (F). Cut 18 strips of thin plywood measuring 16 x 1 inch (400 x 25mm). Use a tenon saw and miter box to cut shallow grooves in each strip at intervals of about 1 in (25mm), to mimic roofing tiles.

8 Glue the cladding to the plywood roof, starting from the bottom and overlapping each layer slightly on the one below. Again, make sure the rows are parallel as you go.

9 Finish the gables with the decorative bargeboards (F). These are constructed by drilling a series of ¾ inch (18mm) holes in two pieces of plywood fashioned as shown in figure 9.1. These are then cut in half and the halves joined at right angles.

10 Nail the bargeboards to the gables. Cut out small diamond-shaped finials (F) from scrap plywood and glue them to the fascia boards where they meet to cover the join. Glue the capping piece (G) on top of the roof. Paint the entire chalet structure (except the roof shingles) in your chosen color. Stain the roof shingles with a cedar-colored preservative to make them look authentic. Mount the birdfeeder on a post (H) or hang it from an overhead support.

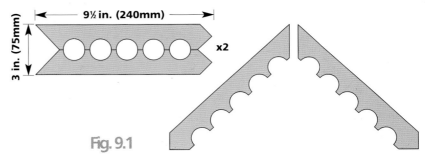

9½ in. (240mm)

3 in. (75mm)

x2

Fig. 9.1

Birdhouse

YOU WILL NEED

Frame (A)
Two hanging baskets with
10 in. (250mm) diameters

Decoration (B)
Plenty of willow shoots, no more than
³⁄₁₆ in. (5mm) thick, but of any length

Hardware and finishing
Short lengths of wire

Chain, clasp, and hook

Tools
Hand pruners, pliers, wire cutters

WORKING WITH WILLOW

To make the weaving as easy as possible, try to use fresh willow. The best time to make these birdhouses is in spring and summer when the willow is supple. If you use it later in the year soak it in lukewarm water until it is pliable.

ALTERNATIVE MATERIALS

Use materials such as rush, rattan, or rope to weave a birdhouse. Also try using different sizes of hanging basket, but avoid ones that are so large that they would look obtrusive.

ATTRACTING SPECIFIC BIRDS

Alter the size of the opening to suit the types of birds you want to attract and position the birdhouse in a location that will suit them. Some species, for example, prefer to nest in secluded areas away from the house.

Simplicity is the key to this delightful willow birdhouse, which has a natural, organic look and is inexpensive to make. "How," your friends will ask, "did you weave willow shoots into such a perfect sphere?" "With great skill," you'll reply, revealing only to your best friends that you built it around a pair of humble hanging baskets. Willow shoots are available in many home supply stores and garden centers, but it's more economical—and much more enjoyable—to cut your own from a tree found growing along a river bank or in another moist area (always ask permission if it's in private grounds!). Hang the birdhouse in a safe and sheltered area of the garden, out of the wind and away from the prying gaze of inquisitive cats.

1 Take the hanging baskets (A) and start weaving willow twigs through the holes. There's no great art to this; just work it out as you go. You may find that it helps to soak even fresh shoots to make them easier to bend.

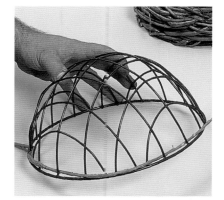

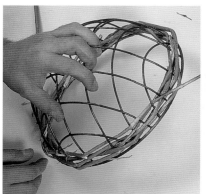

2 Work your way from the edge of the basket towards the bottom. The weave will become tighter and tighter, and you can bulk it up by adding more and more willow. Make sure you completely cover the metal frame with willow shoots.

3 Once you've finished weaving both halves of the basket, join them together with a couple of wire hinges, fixed at opposite sides of the ball. Twist the ends of the wire together with pliers and snip off any sharp pieces with wire cutters.

4 With the baskets securely held together, cut a hole through the willow with hand pruners. Make sure it is the appropriate size for the bird species you would like to attract.

5 For extra security, add another wire tie directly under the hole.

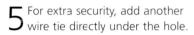

6 Fasten a clasp at one end of the chain and a hook at the other. Attach the clasp to the top of the basket and hang it in the garden.

▶ *As well as attracting birds to your garden, the willow ball makes a delightful piece of rustic sculpture.*

Dovecote

YOU WILL NEED

Main body (A)
One 4 x 8 ft. (1200 x 2400mm) sheet of ¾ in. (18mm) marine plywood

Internal dividers (B)
Two 11¼ x 24½ (280 x 615mm) pieces of ½ in. (12mm) marine plywood

Roof joists (C)
Three 12 in. (300mm) 1 x 2 softwood

Roof (D)
Four roof tiles

Lead flashing and appropriate adhesive, or black exterior sealant

Hardware and finishing
Exterior wood glue

About fifteen 1½ in. (40mm) #8 galvanized screws for assembling sides and roof joists

About forty 1½ in. (40mm) galvanized finishing nails

Exterior wood filler

Four 2 in. (50mm) flap hinges and screws

Two door catches and screws

Four mirror brackets and screws

Wood preservative, paint, stain, varnish

Tools
Basic tool kit plus metal snips, corner clamp and flat file

Doves are welcome visitors to any yard or garden. They'll arrive on their own, but are more likely to stay if they can move into a dovecote, a little house designed just for them.

Building a dovecote sounds challenging but this one is relatively straightforward to make. It is fashioned almost entirely from sheet material, which makes it quite weighty, but it involves little cutting, and you could ask your lumber merchant to do most of this when you buy the wood.

Once doves have settled into their new home you'll need to clean out the compartments periodically to keep the plywood from rotting. The hinged front allows easy access. Happy cooing!

▶ *This traditional white dovecote has been painted green inside, which helps to emphasize the shapes of the windows and add extra visual interest.*

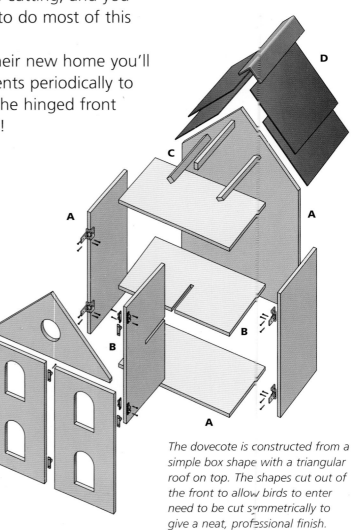

The dovecote is constructed from a simple box shape with a triangular roof on top. The shapes cut out of the front to allow birds to enter need to be cut symmetrically to give a neat, professional finish.

1 From the sheet of plywood (A), cut two sides measuring 12 x 26 in. (300 x 650mm) and a top and a bottom measuring 12 x 24½ in. (300 x 615mm). Clamp together, side pieces outermost, with a corner clamp and drill and countersink two holes at each joint.

2 With the components clamped up, screw them together. Repeat on the remaining sides. If you don't have access to a corner clamp you'll need an assistant to help you with this stage.

3 The two dividers (B) are joined by a halving joint. Cut a slot the thickness of the plywood halfway through one divider from the front of the sheet and halfway through the other divider from the back. Mark the slot carefully and cut inside the lines. Clean up any waste from the end of the slot with a chisel.

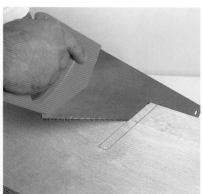

4 The joint should slide together snugly, but sometimes it can be a bit tight. If that's the case, find the tight spot and file it back a little. You will be surprised how little you have to remove to get a smooth fit.

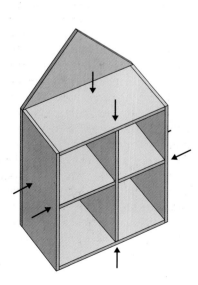

Fig. 5.1

5 Insert the dividers inside the box so that they fit snugly but not tightly. On the outside, mark a line to show where you need to nail through into the dividers (fig 5.1). Remember to tap the nailheads below the surface with a nail set. The box should now be quite sturdy.

6 From the sheet of plywood (A), cut out the back piece, a 26 x 26 inch (650 x 650mm) square with a 13 inch (325mm) tall triangle on top. Use this piece as a template to mark and cut a similar shaped piece for the front. Glue and nail the back piece onto the box assembly. Mark a line ¾ inch (18mm) below the base of the triangle on the front piece and cut along it. Cut the remaining rectangle in half to form the two doors. Mark a 4 inch (100mm) circle at the center of the front triangle, drill a pilot hole and cut out a circle with a jigsaw.

DOVECOTE COLORS

Dovecotes are often painted white, but there's no rule. You could stain your dovecote a color and then varnish it or just varnish the plywood as it is.

LEAD FLASHING

Using metal snips, cut a 3½ x 15 inch (90 x 375mm) piece of lead flashing. Bend it in half lengthwise by placing it on a scrap piece of 4 x 4 wood and bending the flashing over the corner of the wood. Press a piece of scrap batten on top of the flashing to achieve as sharp an angle as possible. Place the flashing on the apex of the roof so that it overhangs slightly at the front. Snip the center of the overhang, then bend back each side of the flashing so that it tucks neatly under the roof tiles. Remove the flashing and apply adhesive to its underside, then attach it to the dovecote.

7 Screw the three roof joists (C) to the backboard triangle. These help to hold the front section in place and support the roof. Position the central joist at the apex of the roof and the others halfway down each side, with their wider sides parallel to the roof angle.

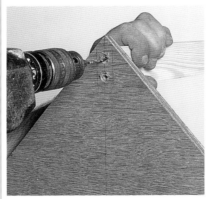

9 Cut the roof tiles (D) if necessary so that they sit flush with the back of the dovecote but overhang the front by about 1 inch (25mm). Nail the tiles to the joists. To protect the apex of the roof, either dress it with lead flashing (see sidebar) or apply an exterior sealant.

8 Now glue and nail the front triangle to the top edge of the box and to the front edge of the roof joists. Once again, use a nail set to sink the heads below the surface so you can fill with wood filler before varnishing or painting.

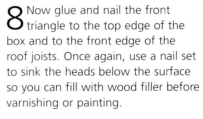

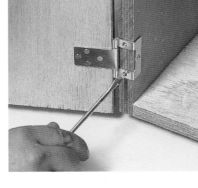

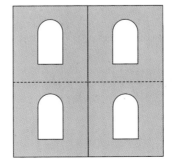

Fig. 10.1

10 Mark the openings on the doors to the appropriate size for doors in your area—the exact dimensions are not critical as long as they are symmetrical (fig. 10.1) and allow doves to enter and exit easily, while not allowing predators inside. Cut the openings out with a jigsaw, then sand the edges smooth. Use a pair of flap hinges to attach each door to the sides of the dovecote. Install catches on the inside to keep the doors shut. Screw mirror brackets to the back of the dovecote to attach it to a wall. Apply wood preservative and paint the dovecote with white paint, then complete the traditional look by painting the architectural detail on the front.

WIDER USE OF GARDEN

FUN

RELAXATION

PURPOSEFUL PLANTING

PLANTS FOR MAKING TEA

Various plants make wonderful tea, either iced or hot.

Blue giant hyssop (*Agastache foeniculum*)

Costmary (*Tanacetum balsamita*)

Garden chamomile (*Chamaemelum nobile*)

Lovage (*Levisticum officinale*)

Southernwood (*Artemisia abrotanum*)

TREES FOR CLIMBING

Children need trees with low branches that can be easily climbed. The best trees have some horizontal branches that can also be used for hanging swings. Conifers are unsuitable because of the spiky leaves and dusty canopy. Trees with spreading branches are best for treehouses.

Cedar of Lebanon (*Cedrus libani*)

Cherry laurel (*Prunus laurocerasus*)

Chestnut (*Castanea* spp.)

Cork oak (*Quercus suber*)

Mock plane (*Acer pseudoplatanus*)

Mulberry trees (*Morus* spp.)

Various willows (*Salix* spp.)

PLANTS WITH RELAXING SMELLS

Time spent lounging in the yard can be improved yet further by the sweet smell of flowering plants, especially those with soporific properties that help you snooze.

- Lavender (*Lavandula spica*) helps you sleep.
- Peppermint (*Mentha* spp.) is a delicious addition to refreshments.
- Common anise (*Pimpinella anisum*) adds flavor to drinks.

Lavender

- The oils produced from the roots of valerian (*Valerian officinalis*) are used to make perfume and are very soporific.

◀ *A large parasol looks striking and provides plenty of shade so that you can relax in your garden comfortably and safely even in strong sunshine.*

Leisure

Some people don't own a lounge chair. Their time in the yard is spent weeding, propagating and maintaining plants and the lawn. A quick glass of iced tea is the nearest they get to relaxing outdoors. But for the rest of us, we look to our garden furniture for horizontal support as we rest beside the pool or watch the kids playing. Lounge chairs, porch swings, rockers and hammocks are all essential items for long leisurely days enjoying the sun.

Come evening, the lights go on and you turn on the heater, depending on the climate and season, to enjoy your garden for a few hours longer. With the children's climbing frame and fort quiet, you can enjoy the dusk and nighttime in peace, recovering from a day of games and fun.

ENJOYING YOUR YARD

Finding a balance between a beautiful garden and a yard that you and your family can enjoy isn't always easy. Children and adults do not necessarily share the same priorities and demands. But with a little imagination, young and old can enjoy the yard and find their own special space for leisure.

- Do you want to enjoy your garden at all times of day? A shady spot will help in the heat of the day, but solar or low-voltage lights let you spend time outdoors in the evenings, and heaters can keep you warm in the moonlight.
- Do you want a bright, fun-filled yard or something more subtle? Plastic children's toys are usually made in vibrant colors that stimulate energy and enthusiasm and are designed to be very safe. But these toys can be too bright for some yards, so wooden climbing frames, forts and treehouses might be more suitable.
- Do you want movement and ornament in the yard? Consider wind chimes and weather vanes. Salvage yards are excellent places to find unusual sculptures and garden accents.

◀ *Sundials are a highly decorative addition to the garden, with stone and metal being the most popular materials.*

Types of Feature

There's more to a garden than weeding and mowing. Get the main work done during the winter and you can dedicate summer to enjoying the results. Buy or build a swing, furnish the yard with games and activities for adults and children and light up the borders for evenings outdoors.

ROCKING AND SWINGING

A porch swing with an awning is a relaxing place to wind down at the end of the day or during the day if you're fortunate enough to enjoy that luxury. You can find one in wood or in metal and fabric. Many are metal-framed, with a fabric covering and even an awning to keep you cool. Some incorporate technology aimed at achieving the best swing. The more sophisticated versions have motors to keep you swinging without any effort. Decide whether to buy a swing for one, two or three people.

For the simplest in swinging comfort, you can't beat the rocker, which is now available in Adirondack style. Getting the right rock is a real skill. The center of balance shouldn't be too far forward or too far back. Test a rocker before buying to ensure it suits your body size and rocking style!

Finding a pair of trees has always been the great challenge for anyone who wants a hammock. You can attach one end to a building and the other to a tree, but a hammock stand gives you the ultimate freedom to follow the sun or the shade. Old-fashioned string hammocks often become threadbare and sad specimens, but they are no longer the only options. Now you can buy designs in a multitude of colors, patterns and fabrics. Cotton will take longer to dry after rain, but it's more comfortable and hugs your body.

▲ This ingenious seating solution combines shade with a pair of swinging seats.

◄ Wooden porch swings are available in different sizes to suit the space you have.

▲ ▶ *The traditional string hammock (above) looks best suspended between two conveniently positioned trees, but hammock stands are available if this is not possible in your garden. For the ultimate in leisure lounging, nothing can beat a wooden and fabric hammock (top right).*

◀ ▶ *A porch rocker (left) is ideal if a fixed swing is too permanent and cumbersome for your space. For the ultimate in versatility, a freestanding swing with canopy (right) lets you enjoy any part of your garden with the maximum of comfort.*

ORNAMENTAL FEATURES

An extraordinary variety of musical wind chimes, weather vanes and sundials can add interest to your yard. Wind chimes can be hung from the porch, as can stained-glass decorations and hanging baskets.

Junkyards or recycling depots often have objects that can be placed around the yard. Obviously these are often in a classical style, but there's plenty of scope for more dramatic effects and imaginative use of rejects. The most unlikely objects—old cars or even farm equipment—have been used to create striking effects as outdoor decoration. Visitors enjoy the surprise of finding an unlikely feature in hidden corners of a yard, while old statues draped with climbing plants give the garden a period feel, like ruins overtaken by the jungle.

◄ ► *Introducing sound into your garden can revolutionize its atmosphere. These wind chimes are designed in a variety of sizes to produce different sounds (left). Add some sparkle to a quiet corner of your yard with a decorative sundial (right).*

▼ ► *Weather vanes (below) abound in junkyards and add a quirky touch to an outdoor space. Treehouses (right) are a firm favorite with children, whether simple arboreal playhouses or complex feats of carpentry.*

CHILDREN'S ACTIVITIES

Although you can find mass-produced games and activities for children—including trampolines, swings and wading pools—the most interesting are often produced by local craftspeople. You can usually find someone to build a treehouse, an adventure climbing frame, or a fort, customized to your own specific requirements.

But you can't predict what children will or will not enjoy. Many an expensive playhouse is rejected in favor of a battered old shed. Young children need attention, obviously, and like to be watched, so make sure the activities suit the part of your yard you'd normally frequent. Otherwise you'll spend your time far from where you like to sit, eat and lounge. Wood is a popular material for children's activities because it looks better than plastic on a lawn, is child-friendly (as long as there are no splinters), and will last the few years it's needed.

Swings come in many styles, from simple seats on chain or rope

▲ If you have the space, an integrated play system incorporating swings, den, slide and climbing frames will give your children hours of fun.

to swinging plastic gondolas. Frames for swings need to be solid enough not to rock. Dig the wooden poles into the ground or hold them down with pegs. Check before you buy to see how well the swings work, making sure they don't yaw out of line. Put them on chopped bark chips or rubber matting for safety's sake; otherwise you'll end up with muddy patches where the grass is worn away, and mowing around the frames is always a challenge.

You can buy slides for fastening to frames or onto a low tree. Fruit trees, with the heart pruned away, make ideal supports for a slide, because children can climb a ladder on one side, work their way through the tree and slide down the other side. Watch out, though, for stinging insects once the fruit starts to ripen.

Naturally, dens and treehouses can be hidden as the children get older and want their independence. They will begin wanting to build their own refuge and will value your skills with a saw and hammer to create somewhere for them to hide.

▼ This play system features bright primary colors that young children will like, but you could choose a natural wood version to blend more subtly with your garden.

◀ ▲ Dens and playhouses (at left) look great and are available in a wide price range. Sturdy trees are the perfect support for children's swings, such as this one made from an old tire (above).

HEATERS

Depending on where you live, outside heating may be necessary for evenings in the yard, especially during spring and fall. The most popular heat sources are gas stoves that radiate heat with metal deflectors, usually from above. These are relatively mobile and can offer good heat, though it is localized, which can mean guests at one end of a table are being roasted while others, farther away, freeze.

A more natural alternative is the chimenea. This is usually made from pottery, in a rustic style, and is basically an outdoor oven with an opening at the front for lighting the fire and cooking food and a chimney above to radiate heat.

◄ ▲ Outdoor gas heaters are becoming increasingly popular in domestic settings. Their only real drawback is that the heat is rather localized.

LIGHTING

Paraffin lamps, that can't be blown out by wind, are an ideal alternative to candlelight, although there are now breeze-proof candle holders that can be hung from a terrace or on posts. Security lights are inexpensive and powerful for lighting up an eating area or a specific piece of garden furniture. These can be set to stay on all the time or when the sensor picks up movement. Lights are great for highlighting a particular tree or other garden features like bridges or wells. Indeed, a light set inside a decorative well makes a superb centerpiece, while the well itself offers extra seating. Instead of a light, you could install a small pump and create a water cascade in the center of the well.

▲ ▼ A chimenea—a clay oven used for cooking food and providing heat—makes an attractive addition to any garden (above). Wall-mounted heaters (below) warm like the sun allowing you to enjoy your garden in the evening.

SOLAR LIGHTING

The power of the sun comes into its own at night, when the batteries in solar lanterns are  *automatically turned on. The joy of solar lights and pumps in ponds is that you can move them around without worrying about wires.*

Q How do solar lights work?

A Solar panels store power in small batteries. The light can be turned on manually or with a sensor when it gets dark.

Q Will they light up the garden?

A No. Solar lights give small pools of light. They don't have the power to illuminate your yard.

Q Does it matter where you place the lights?

A If you position a solar lamp in the center of the yard, away from any shade, the power might last up to eight hours at night. Put it in shade and you'll lose anything from one to three hours of illumination—on a dull winter's day lack of light will only generate enough energy for a couple of hours' light at night. Nearby spotlights can turn off solar lights, so you must place them at least 5 yards (5m) from strong electric light.

Q How does the quality of solar panels differ?

A Amorphous panels need sunlight, not just daylight. These are usually in cheaper solar lamps and are the least efficient. You can find solar lamps of up to 8 watts, but the cheapest ones store only half a watt of power.

Q How do you position the lights?

A Many of them have spikes to make positioning very simple. You can also buy lamps that hang from poles or are built into cabinets. Design varies from period reproduction to avant-garde.

Q What's the alternative to solar power?

A You can tap the building's electricity by running cables underground in protective sheathing. An easier option for bright lighting is to attach lamps or spotlights to walls, with cables connected to the interior supply. A safer solution is to use 12 volt lights, which can provide good illumination but don't require a high level of safety protection.

▲ ▶ *Lights placed inside freestanding posts can be located wherever you require nighttime lighting in your garden and are available in both traditional and modern designs.*

▲ *No matter how big or small your garden, you can really use your imagination with water features, whether you opt for an elaborate bridge, a decorative well that is lit from the inside or a miniature pond and fountain.*

Child's Fort

YOU WILL NEED

Floor (A)
One 4 x 8 ft. (1200 x 2400mm) sheet of ¾ in. (19mm) marine plywood

Flooring joists (B)
Five 39 in. (1000mm) 2 x 4 sawn softwood

Two 96 in. (2400mm) 2 x 4 sawn softwood

High wall frames (C)
Six 43 in. (1090mm) 2 x 3 softwood for the middle and end horizontal fixings

Four 43¾ in. (1110mm) 2 x 3 softwood for the side horizontal fixings

Fifteen 28 in. (700mm) 2 x 3 softwood for the vertical fixings

Low wall frames (D)
Four 43¾ in. (1110mm) 2 x 3 softwood for the horizontal fixings

Six 22 in. (560mm) 2 x 3 softwood for the vertical fixings

Wall panels (E)
Four 4 x 8 ft. (1200 x 2400mm) sheets of ¾ in. (19mm) marine plywood

Ladder sides (F)
Two 68 in. (1700mm) 2 x 3 softwood

Ladder rungs (G)
One 120 in. (3000mm) 2 x 2 softwood

Posts (H)
Six 108 in. (2700mm) 4 x 4 pressure-treated softwood fence posts

Capping pieces (I)
Two 43¾ in. (1110mm) 1 x 4 softwood

Hardware and finishing
Forty 4 in. (100mm) #12 galvanized screws to assemble floor joists and screw to posts

One hundred and twenty-six 3 in. (75mm) #10 galvanized screws to assemble wall frames and screw to posts

Forty 1½ in. (40mm) #8 galvanized screws to attach ladder rungs, to screw floor to joists and for capping pieces

Eighty 1½ in. (40mm) galvanized nails to attach the wall panels to the frames

Six 4 x 4 in. (100mm) post bases to secure the posts in concrete

Wood preservative, paint, stain, varnish

Tools
Basic tool kit plus circular saw

Children of all ages love outdoor play structures, and this versatile fort is sure to become a favorite family play area. With just a little imagination, it will be transformed into a cowboy's cabin, medieval castle, princess's palace or even a haunted house.

The fort is freestanding so you can put it anywhere, with its supporting posts either set in deep holes or attached to concrete slabs with post holders bolted to the concrete. As with all children's toys, take extra care when finishing to make sure there are no sharp edges or areas where fingers can get pinched. If your lawn dries out in the summer, consider surrounding the fort with shock-absorbing matting to protect against injury in case of a fall.

The entire fort is built around a single piece of ¾ inch (19mm) marine plywood, which is used for the floor and acts as a template for everything else. The floor is supported by a framework of joists screwed to the posts, and notched to fit around them. The vertical side frames that form the walls are screwed to the floor and the posts, and covered with plywood sides.

▶ *This classic raised fort will provide hours of enjoyment, but there is a balance to be struck between safety and adventurous play. While the fort is suitable for children aged 3–8, younger children require supervision.*

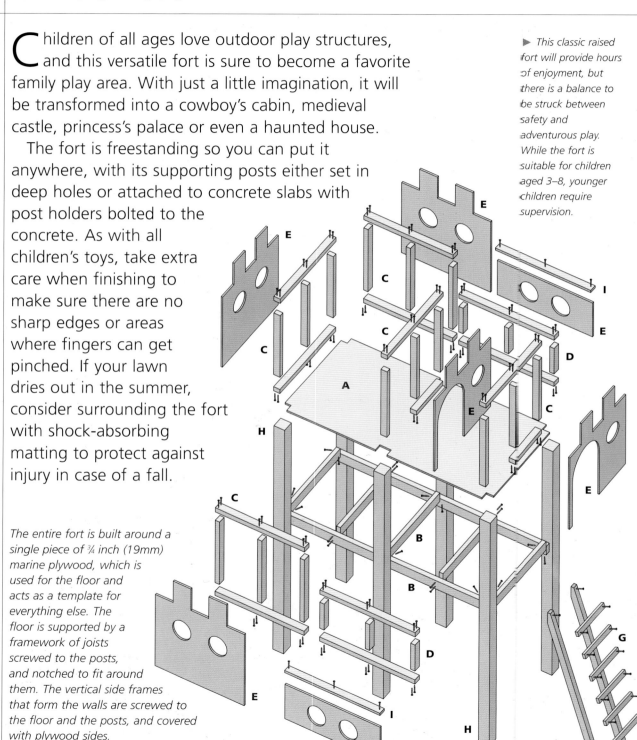

1 Mark 2½ inch (62mm) square notches in the corners of the plywood floor (A) for the posts. The fact that the dressed posts are 1 inch (25mm) larger than the notches leaves space for the ¾ inch (19mm) plywood that you will attach to the side frames (fig. 1.1).

2 The notch at the center of each side is also 2½ inches (62mm) deep, but 3½ inches (87mm) wide. Again, this leaves a 1 inch (25mm) space for the side frames. Cut out all the notches with a jigsaw. Remember that this floor will help determine the position of the posts, so the cuts must be accurate.

3 Screw the long and the short flooring joists (B) together to make the subframe that supports the plywood floor. Lay the joists on the floor to position them accurately. The short joists are equally spaced; the end joists flush with the ends of the floor; and the entire frame sits inside the notches.

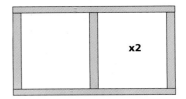

Fig. 5.1

23 in. (585mm)

x2

Front and central high wall frames

Fig. 6.1

x2

Low wall frames

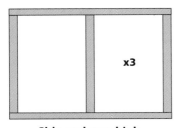

post   2½ in. (62mm)

Fig. 1.1

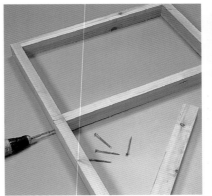

x3

Side and rear high wall frames

Fig. 4.1

4 Screw together the side and rear high wall frames (C) as shown in fig 4.1. The ends of the horizontal frame members are flush with the sides of the vertical members at each end and the third vertical member is centered between the two. Note that the side frames, at 43¾ inches (1110mm), are fractionally longer than the rear frame, which is 43 inches (1090mm) long.

5 Screw together the front and central high wall frames (C). The wall panels that are attached to these will have archways cut in their left-hand sides, so the central frame member is offset slightly to the right. Position it 23 inches (585mm) from the left-hand vertical fixing (fig. 5.1). Note also that the lower horizontal fixing will be cut away later (Step 9) for ease of access.

6 Now screw together the low wall frames (D), which fence in the area at the top of the ladder. As with the side and rear high wall frames, the inner fixing is centered (fig. 6.1). Once you have assembled all the wall frames, check to see that they fit neatly inside the notches in the plywood floor. They will ultimately be screwed to the posts and covered with the wall panels.

SLATTED SIDES

Instead of using plywood sides on the fort, you could use wooden slats. Slatted walls might suit some garden designs better than plywood. The softwood used for them also weathers better than plywood.

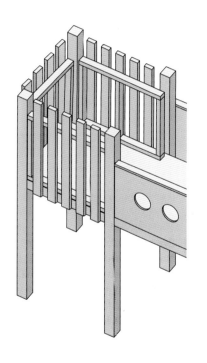

7 Measure and mark the plywood for the wall panels (E), starting with the five high ones. The panels at the ends of the fort and the one in the center measure 43 inches (1090mm) wide by 45 inches (1140mm) high, allowing for the battlements to be cut out and for the panels to overhang the floor and the joists. The high panels at the sides measure 43¾ inches (1110mm) wide by 45 inches (1143mm) high. Now mark each of the two low wall panels—43¾ inches (1110mm) wide by 29½ inches (750mm) high, which will again allow them to overhang the floor and joists. Cut each wall panel out neatly with a circular saw so it will fit between the notches and posts.

8 Once the wall panels are cut, mark the battlements for the high walls. Make the battlements and the spaces between and either side of them about 8½ inches (216mm) wide by 9½ inches (240mm) deep—a balanced appearance is more important than exact dimensions. Mark the first panel, shading the waste, then cut it out with a jigsaw. When you are satisfied with the shape, use this panel to mark the others.

10 Use your compass to mark circles for the portholes. Cut them out of all the wall panels. It's best to keep the diameter of the portholes to 6 inches or less, to prevent the possibility of a little head getting stuck in one of them! Cut out the arches and portholes with a jigsaw, drilling access holes first. You can then sand and prime all seven panels and paint them as desired.

9 Mark the arches on the front and central wall panel 20 inches (510mm) wide by 30 inches (765mm) high. Take care to position them centrally between the middle and left-hand frame members. Make a simple string-and-pencil compass to mark the curve at the top of the archway. Hammer in a nail 10 inches (255mm) from the top of the archway and the same distance from the side. Attach a 10 inch (255mm) length of string with a pencil at the end and mark the curve.

SETTING POSTS IN CONCRETE

We have chosen to bolt the posts into post bases set in concrete slabs because it makes building the fort relatively easy. This method allows you to build the fort and put it into position at the last moment. Forts built around posts sunk into the ground, on the other hand, must be braced while you build the subframe, floor and side frames. If you decide to work this way, nail thin strapping pieces to the posts and push them into the ground to keep the posts in position while you build the fort.

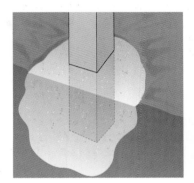

Fig. 13.1

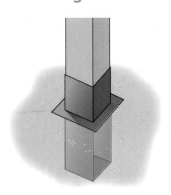

11 Now make the ladder. Use a combination square to mark a taper of 30 degrees at the end of one ladder side (F). Cut the taper with a handsaw. Use this piece to mark the taper on the other side of the ladder and cut it out.

12 With the ladder sides clamped together, mark the positions for the six rungs (G), making sure they are spaced equally apart. Cut six 20-inch (500mm) lengths of 2 x 2 and sand the ends. Drill the rungs, counterboring with a spade bit so you will be able to glue the plugs in later. Screw the rungs to the sides. Glue the plugs in place, let the glue set and sand the plugs for a smooth finish. Now you're ready to assemble the fort in the yard.

14 Once the subframe is fixed in place, remove the temporary battens. Lift the floor onto the frame and screw it to the joists at regular intervals, countersinking the screws. Next screw the wall frames to the posts and to the floor. Use two countersunk screws through each vertical fixing and two through each horizontal fixing into the floor and flooring joist below.

Fig. 13.2

13 Prepare and level an area of ground. Lay the plywood floor on the ground and mark the positions of the post holes. Dig the holes, 12 inches (300mm) in diameter and 30 inches (760mm) deep, or to the frost depth in your area, and fill with concrete. Push the post bases into the concrete so that the lower portion of the base is submerged and the base plate is flush with the surface. When the concrete has set, insert the posts in the bases and fix following the manufacturers' instructions. Screw temporary battens to the posts so their top edges are 63 inches (1600mm) from the ground (fig. 13.2). Get an assistant to help you lift the subframe onto the battens. Screw it to the posts using two angled screws in each corner. At the central posts, screw from each side of the central short joist, again at a slight angle.

LIFTING THE ROOF

For a year-round fort, you can add a roof. The simple way to do this is by screwing strapping to the inside of the plywood panels or by making the wall frames high enough to attach a plywood roof to them. Make sure the roof is pitched so that rain and snow will run off. If you are making a cowboy cabin, you can give it a sloping shed roof as shown in the lower drawing. Or, if you are feeling ambitious, you could make an arched roof over curved plywood sections or use the techniques described in the Arbor project on page 120 for making a pitched roof. Cover the roof with roll roofing to protect it from the elements.

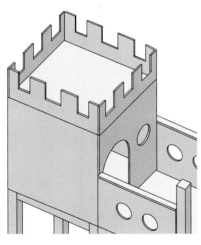

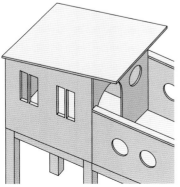

15 Nail the wall panels to the corresponding frames using three nails for each side of each panel, except for the vertical sides of the lower wall panels, where two per side should suffice. Punch the nails below the surface with a nail set and then fill the holes. Paint over the filler when it is dry.

17 Now that the structure is secure, saw away the exposed parts of the wall frames in the two archways, taking care not to saw through the floor or the wall panels.

16 Screw the capping pieces (J) to the tops of the wall frames on the two low walls using four equally spaced countersunk screws on each side. The capping pieces are slightly wider than the combined thickness of the wall frames and the wall panels, so you can either make them flush with the inside edge of the wall or equalize the space on either side. Fill the screw holes and finish the capping pieces as desired.

18 Attach the ladder to the front of the fort, aligning it with the bottom edge of the archway. Drill and screw through the plywood wall panel and into the flooring joist behind it and counterbore with a spade bit. For extra sturdiness, secure the bottom of the ladder to the ground using security brackets or wooden stakes driven into the ground. Plug the screw holes and apply your chosen finish to the ladder. Drill four (or more) small holes in each corner of the base of the fort in order to let rain drain away.

Hammock Stand

It is surprisingly difficult to find a pair of trees close enough together to hang a hammock; in an orchard, perhaps, but few of us are lucky enough to have one and, in any case, most fruit trees attract bees and wasps. The best solution is a purpose-built hammock stand, one that can be sited wherever you like and even moved to suit the seasons or the time of day.

This stylish contemporary design is made from strong, ¾ inch (18mm) exterior-grade birch plywood. Each support comprises two triangles at right angles to another, leaning away from the hammock to resist the force of gravity. At the foot, a sandwich of cross-braces holds them apart. Hooks for the hammock are attached to the top.

▶ *Try painting just the triangular supports. Choose a relaxing color so that, when you hang the hammock, all you'll want to do is lie back and let your cares slip away.*

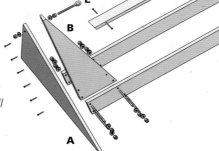

The hammock stand is relatively easy to make from four triangles and three lengths of wood, but the cutting involved can be complicated, so take your time when measuring and marking out. Alternatively give the measurements to your lumber dealer and ask if he'll do the cutting for you.

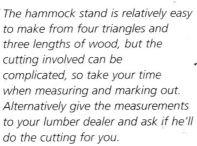

1 Measure and mark out the four triangles for the back (A) and rib supports (B) on the sheet of plywood, as shown in fig. 1.1. Note that triangle A is an isosceles triangle, that is, it is symmetrical on both sides of the midline. With the plywood sheet well supported in several places, carefully cut out all four triangles.

Fig. 1.1

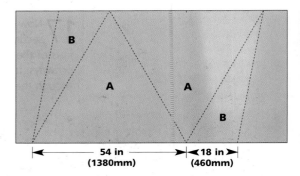

54 in (1380mm)   18 in (460mm)

2 Measure and mark the mid ine on the back supports (A). Mark, drill and countersink six evenly spaced holes along each line, where the back supports will be screwed to the ribs (B). Do not assemble yet.

3 Lay the rib on one of the cross-braces (C), align their bottom edges and trace the angle made by the rear face of the rib on the end of the brace. Extend the line all the way around the piece using a square and ruler, and cut with a saw.

 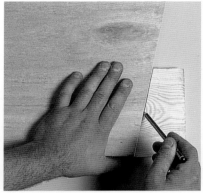 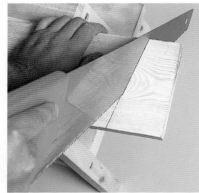

4 Mark and cut the other end of the brace in exactly the same way, then mark and cut both ends of the other cross-brace so it's an identical twin. Now return to the back supports and screw these to the ribs, but do not glue at this stage.

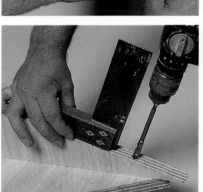 

6 Unscrew the backs and place them on a worksurface. Center a wider spade bit on the small hole created by the tip of the thin spade bit and make a larger, but very shallow, hole in the outside face of the back. This is for the washer and nut that will hold the eyebolt in place. Repeat on the other support. When you complete this operation, the backs may now be permanently glued and screwed to the r ribs.

5 Before joining the two triangular supports with the cross-braces, drill them for the hammock hooks (E). First use a thin countersinking spade bit, entering from the front, at right angles to the leading edge of the rib and about 2½ in. (65mm) down from the apex, stopping a fraction short so that only the tip of the bit breaks through the rear of the back support.

PROVIDING SHADE

Without trees to provide shade, you may want to create your own. You could do this quite simply by integrating a "mast" at each end and attaching a ridge pole between them. Throw a piece of fabric over the pole and spread this out using guy ropes pegged to the ground.

ATTACHING THE HAMMOCK

Tie the hammock to the eyebolts with a clove hitch knot (below). If your hammock has a loop at each end, you could use a carabiner instead. This is an oblong-shaped metal ring with a spring-hinged side that mountaineers use as a secure connector.

7 Use a tenon saw to make the points of the triangles less sharp, and round the edges with a file and sandpaper. Insert the eyebolts and secure each bolt with a washer and nut on both sides.

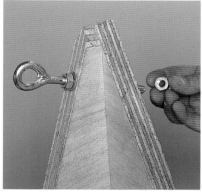

8 Position the cross-braces on both sides of a rib, with their ends butted up against the back support. Hold the assembly together with a clamp, using a scrap of plywood as a spacer. Drill four holes through the cross-braces and the rib for the bolts. Secure each bolt with a nut, using a washer at either end.

10 Fill any countersunk screw heads with wood filler. Then apply wood preservative and your choice of paint, stain and/or varnish. Remember to remove the hammock hooks before you do so.

9 Carefully position the cover strip (C) over the cross-braces and against the rib. Use a bevel square to find the angle made between the cover strip and rib. Mark this angle on the end of the cover strip and saw to fit so that it will sit flush against the rib. Attach the cross-braces to the opposite rib as described in Step 8. Check the required length for the cover strip, cut it to size and angle the end as before. Drill, countersink and screw the strip to the cross members, using four equally spaced screws along each side of the strip.

Swing Bench

YOU WILL NEED

Seat formers and rails (A)
One 48 x 96 in. (1200 x 2400mm) sheet of ¾ in. (19mm) marine plywood

Thin seat slats (B)
Approximately twenty-eight 50 in. (1270mm) pieces of 1 x 1 in. softwood

Wide seat slats (C)
Approximately eighteen 50 in. (1270mm) pieces of 1 x 2 in. softwood

Legs (D)
Four 82 in. (2080mm) 2 x 4 softwood

Cross bearers (E)
Two 33 in. (835mm) 2 x 4 softwood

Capping piece (F)
One 96 in. (2440mm) 2 x 6 softwood

Beam (G)
One 90 in. (2290mm) 2 x 4 softwood

Vertical supports (H)
Two 38 in. (965mm) 2 x 2 softwood

Diagonal brackets (I)
Four 28 in. (710mm) 1 x 4 softwood

Vertical facings (J)
Two 41½ in. (1050mm) 1 x 4 softwood

Hardware and finishing
Eight 4 in. (100mm) lag screws

Six 2½ in. (60mm) lag screws

About one hundred and fifty 1½ in. (40mm) finish nails for attaching the seat slats to the formers.

Two 8 in. (200mm) M12 eyebolts

Four 4 in. (100mm) M12 eyebolts with locking nuts

Twenty-four 2 in. (50mm) #10 galvanized screws for assembling the A-frame

Eight 1¾ in. (45mm) #8 galvanized screws to join the formers and rails

Five 3 in. (75mm) #10 galvanized screws to attach the capping piece to the beam

Four ½ in. (13mm) hardwood plugs

26 ft. (8m) of thick, strong rope

Exterior wood glue

Wood preservative, paint, stain, varnish

Tools
Basic tool kit plus compass, mallet, wrench

This swing bench can be hung from an A-frame, as shown here, or you can attach it to a beam on a veranda or porch. The lines have been kept very simple, and the seat slats are thin enough for a bit of give to make it even more comfortable as you swing. The bench is constructed on plywood formers screwed to plywood rails. The central former is joined to the rails with cross halving joints for extra rigidity. To keep things as simple as possible, the curves of the formers are based around a series of four circles, three of which have the same radius. Only the top back curve is tighter.

▶ *With its restful rocking motion and ergonomic contours, this swing bench is the ultimate in outdoor relaxation.*

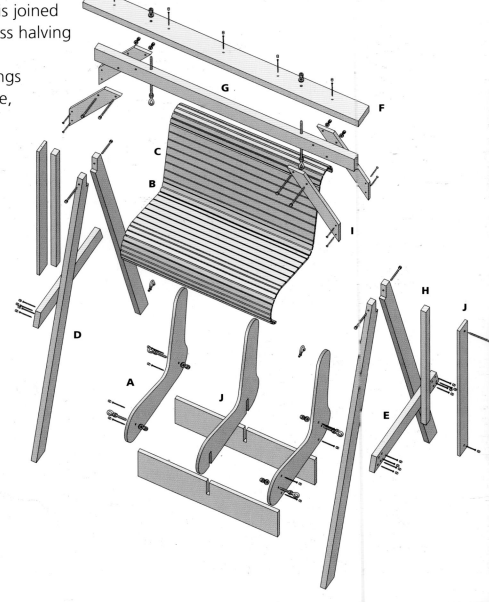

1 Cut two rails 47¼ inches (1200mm) wide by 7 inches (180mm) deep from the plywood. In one corner mark a square measuring 27½ inches (700mm) by 24 inches (610mm). Set a compass to a radius of 4 inches (100mm) and in the bottom left corner of the square draw a circle (i) that touches the bottom and left edges of the square.

2 Use the completed former as a template to draw the other two. Cut these out, and clamp the three formers together to mark the position of the rails, 5 inches (130mm) from each end of the formers. The central former has a cross-halving joint. Mark the position for the screw holes on the outer formers.

3 Drill ½ inch (13mm) holes through the centers of circles (i) and (ii) on the two outer formers. These holes are for the eyebolts, which will serve as location points for the rope. Clamp the two formers together so that you can drill both holes at once.

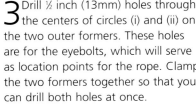

Fig. 6.1

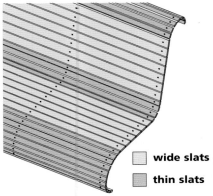

wide slats
thin slats

Draw a similar circle (ii) in the bottom right-hand corner of the square. Reset the compass to 2½ inches (65mm) and draw a circle (iii) in the top right-hand corner. Draw line X from the center of circle (ii) touching the edge of circle (i). Draw line Y at 90 degrees to line X touching the edge of circle (iii). Draw circle (iv) touching lines X and Y. Cut out around the bold line (fig. 1.1).

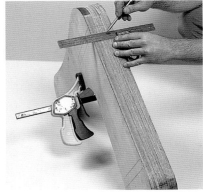

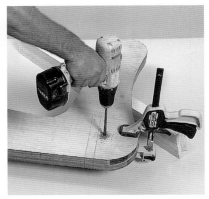

Fig. 1.1

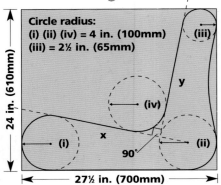

Circle radius:
(i) (ii) (iv) = 4 in. (100mm)
(iii) = 2½ in. (65mm)

24 in. (610mm)

(iii)

y

(iv)

(i)

x

90°

(ii)

27½ in. (700mm)

4 Working from the marks made in Step 2, mark the cross-halving joint in the central former. Make the cuts 2 inches (50mm) deep and ¾ inch (19mm) wide, sawing down the sides of the joint and chiseling out the waste. Cut joints exactly the same size, dead center in the two rails.

5 Slot together the central former and rails (they don't need to be glued) and offer up the outer formers one at a time to check to see that the marks you made earlier for screw holes line up with the ends of the rails. Once you're satisfied with the fit, drill, glue and screw the outer formers to the rails. Counterbore the holes with a ½ inch (13mm) spade bit for plugging at a later stage.

6 Carefully lay out the seat slats (B and C) on the three formers, the thin slats following the curves and the wide ones on the straight sections (fig. 6.1). Begin to nail the slats to the formers, starting at the rear of the seat and using a couple of ¼ inch (6mm) spacers to regularize the gaps. Tap the nail heads below the surface with a nail set. Turn the seat on its back to nail the slats to the back.

SHADY SOLUTIONS

Siting the swing bench under a tree provides you with automatic shade, but an alternative is to add an awning to the A-frame. The simplest way to do this is to attach fabric to the beam, supporting it at the front with poles held in place with guy ropes. You can use any type of thick material, such as canvas, sailcloth or a synthetic fabric.

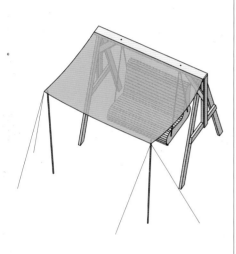

7 Finish nailing the seat slats in place. Glue and plug the screw holes in the formers. When the glue has dried, trim the protruding ends of the plugs flush with a chisel, ensuring that the plugs don't split away below the surface. Sand smooth.

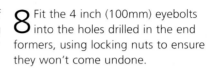
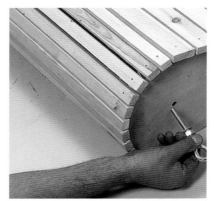

8 Fit the 4 inch (100mm) eyebolts into the holes drilled in the end formers, using locking nuts to ensure they won't come undone.

9 Now begin work on the A-frame. The simplest way to work out the angled cuts at the top and bottom of the legs (D), and the notch to house the beam (G), is to mark out half the frame full size on a piece of plywood as shown in fig. 9.1. Use this as a template to cut both legs.

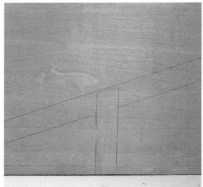

10 Lay the legs in position on the ground and verify that the legs meet at the top, and that the notch will house the beam. Lay the cross bearers on the legs as shown in fig 9.1, mark their position on the legs and mark the trim angle on their ends. Cut to size with a handsaw.

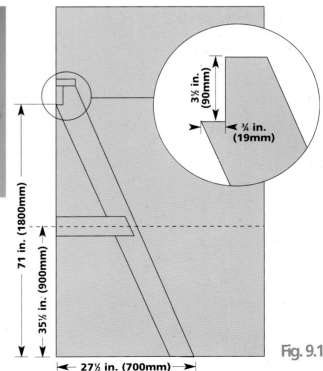

3½ in. (90mm)

¾ in. (19mm)

71 in. (1800mm)

35½ in. (900mm)

27½ in. (700mm)

Fig. 9.1

ALTERNATIVE HANGING FRAME

If you'd rather not build the A-frame, you could simply sink a couple of heavy posts into the ground, with a beam between them to support the bench.

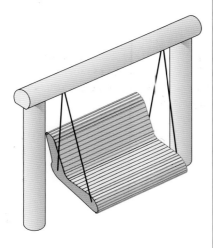

11 Drill, glue, and screw the cross bearers into place on each of the A-frame sides. Drill holes in the top of each leg for the lag screws that fix the legs to the beam, positioned so the screws will not hit each other when screwed in. Screw and glue the capping piece (F) to the beam (G), centered on the beam and with an equal amount of overhang at each end. It's easier to do this now, before the beam is attached to the A-frame.

12 Prepare and level a suitable site. Take the sides of the frame to the site you have chosen. Final assembly is best carried out on site as the construction is awkward to move once assembled. Get a friend or two to help you hold the legs while you drop the beam and capping piece into the notches. Screw the legs to the beam with the 4 inch (100mm) lag screws.

13 Measure the distance from the underside of the capping piece to the top of the cross bearer beneath and, if necessary, adjust the length of the vertical supports (H) to suit. Drill, countersink, and screw the top of one of the supports to the end of the beam, butted tight against the underside of the capping piece. Use a spirit level to make sure the support is plumb when you attach it.

14 Fix the bottom of the vertical support to the center of the cross bearer, again using a spirit level to make sure it's straight. Drill and countersink a pilot hole, and insert the screw at a shallow angle. Attach the other vertical support in the same way on the other side.

DOUBLE SEATER

If you have enough space to site the swing bench in the middle of the yard, you could make a two-way seat. All you need do is double up the shape of the formers, and use some more slats. Attach the swing rope from eyebolts on both sides of the bench. The design for the bench could also be shortened to make a swing chair.

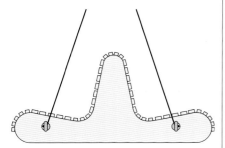

ROCK STEADY

For extra stability, you can stake the bottoms of the A-frame legs into the ground using the method described in the Hexagonal Tree Bench project on page 62.

15 To stop the swing from moving side to side, bolt diagonal brackets (I) to each side of the beam and the vertical supports. Cut the ends of the brackets at 45 degrees. Clamp one pair of brackets to either side of the beam and vertical support, then drill all the way through so that you can attach them with lag screws. Repeat on the other side.

16 Bolt the diagonal brackets to the beam and vertical supports, using the 4 inch (100mm) lag screws.

18 Mark the position for the swing hooks 18 inches (460mm) in from each end of the beam. Drill holes through the beam and capping piece to accept the 8 inch (200mm) eyebolts. Bolt them in place, and screw the swing hooks through the eyes of the bolts. Attach the rope to the hooks with a secure knot, and to the bench at the other end (fig. 18.1). Finally, apply the finish of your choice.

17 Screw the vertical facings (J) to the end of each A-frame side, using a screw at the top and bottom. The top screw needs to go between the two screws you used to attach the vertical support to the beam, so mark the position of these on the facing before drilling and countersinking the hole. The bottom screw is screwed into the cross bearer.

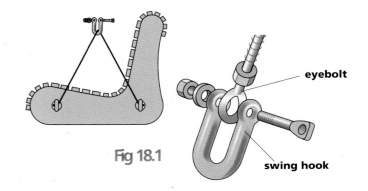

Fig 18.1

eyebolt

swing hook

Weather Vane

YOU WILL NEED

Boat hull (A)
One 12 in. (300mm) 2 x 6 softwood

Mast (B)
One 12 in. (300mm) piece of ⅜ in. (10mm) diameter softwood dowel

Armature rod (C)
One 12 in. (300mm) piece of steel rod to fit bearing

Sails and rigging (D)
Scraps of canvas or other suitable fabric and some string

Post (E)
One 4 x 4 pressure-treated softwood fencepost to a length of your choosing

NSEW markers (F)
Large scrap of ½ in. (12mm) marine plywood

NSEW holders (G)
Two 24in. (600mm) pieces of ⅜ in. (10mm) diameter softwood dowel

Hardware and finishing
Five 1³⁄₁₆ in. (30mm) eyelet screws for attaching the rigging to the boat

Six brass eyelets for attaching the rigging to the sails

Two 1½ in. (38mm) #8 galvanized screws for attaching the bearing unit to the post

Sealed bearing

Exterior grade adhesive

Wood preservative, paint, stain, varnish

Tools
Basic tool kit plus eyelet tool, butterfly bit for attaching the bearing and drill press

Knowing the direction and strength of the wind may not be as important in your yard as it is on a sailboat, but a nautical theme is ideal for a weather vane. The sails on the boat catch the wind, turning the craft to signal its direction. Of course, you can use any design you like as long as it has some sort of "sail" that will show the wind direction.

The key component in this weather vane is a sealed bearing that allows it to rotate easily. Buy a bearing at most good hardware stores or search the internet for a supplier. Once you've located the bearing, buy the armature rod to fit.

▶ *When the wind fills its sails and it tacks around, this little boat will bring the lure of the ocean to your yard, even if you live far inland.*

This weather vane is quite straightforward to construct, but it does require very accurate perpendicular drilling of the mast and armature holes, for which you'll need a drill press.

1 Using the measurements given in fig. 1.1, mark the hull shape (A) on the 2 x 6 board. Either draw the curve for the hull freehand or use a compass. Cut out with a jigsaw and clean up any ragged edges with a sanding block.

2 Using a ⅜ inch (10mm) spade bit, drill a 1 inch (25mm) deep hole for the mast (B), centered on the width and length of the hull. Clamp the hull to a longer piece of wood to hold it while you drill. Turn the hull over and drill another 1 inch (25mm) deep hole in the center of the keel for the armature rod (C), using a spade bit of a diameter that will allow the rod to fit snugly in the hole.

Fig. 1.1

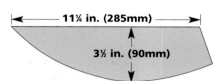

11¼ in. (285mm)

3½ in. (90mm)

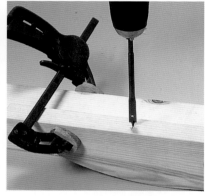

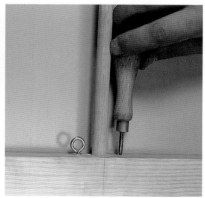

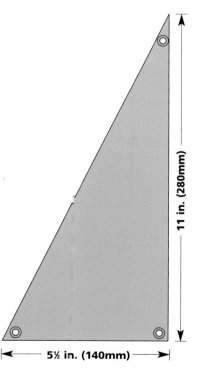

3 Glue the mast into the hull and wipe away any excess glue. If you plan to stain or varnish the hull, do it before you insert the mast.

4 Mark out and cut the canvas for the sails (D), following the measurements given in fig. 4.1. Turn over and glue the edges to prevent the hems from fraying. Punch holes at the corners and attach brass eyelets for securing the sails to the mast. Most craft stores sell inexpensive tool kits to insert eyelets.

5 Attach eyelet screws about ½ inch (12mm) either side of the mast to set the mainsail and jib. Attach another eyelet screw in the top of the mast. You'll need one at the bow and one at the stern of the boat as well. Tie lines made of string to the sails and attach them to the boat. Once the sails are in place, insert the armature rod by pushing it into the keel of the hull.

11 in. (280mm)

5½ in. (140mm)

Fig. 4.1

ADJUSTING THE DESIGN

Any design can be used in combination with the basic concept of a weather vane. Instead of a boat, you could cut out the shape of an athlete, an animal or anything else that will catch the wind and attach it to a bearing with a rod or dowel. Alternatively, instead of attaching NSEW markers to dowels, you could let the markers themselves act as sails. In this case, you would construct the cross pieces with the cross halving joint that's used for the internal compartments of the Dovecote project on page 140. After the adhesive in the joint has set, drill a hole ¾ inch (18mm) deep for the armature and add a design to the top. Here we've made a simple cutout from a piece of ¾ inch (18mm) thick marine plywood.

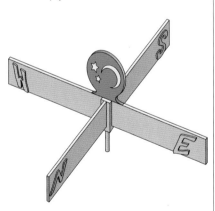

6 The sealed bearing sits in the top of the post (E). Use a flat butterfly bit to drill a wide hole for the bearing. Then drill a smaller hole that is slightly deeper than the bearing to house the armature rod. Position the bearing on the post and set it in place, making sure that it fits tightly in the hole. Note that you may not be able to buy exactly the same bearing as we have used, in which case you may need to adjust some of the measurements and processes.

7 Design then draw the letters for the NSEW markers (F) on a piece of plywood. Use a jigsaw or coping saw to cut them out.

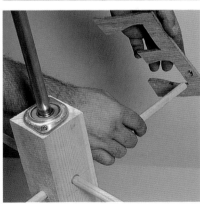
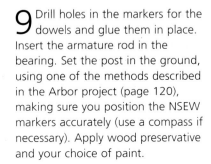

8 To attach the NSEW holders (G), mark a hole in the center of the post about 4 inches (100mm) from the top. Using a ⅜ inch (10mm) bit, drill right through the post. Drill another hole through the center of the adjacent face about 1 inch (25mm) lower than the first. Squirt glue into the holes and insert the dowel rods. Center the rods in the holes and wipe off any excess glue.

9 Drill holes in the markers for the dowels and glue them in place. Insert the armature rod in the bearing. Set the post in the ground, using one of the methods described in the Arbor project (page 120), making sure you position the NSEW markers accurately (use a compass if necessary). Apply wood preservative and your choice of paint.

Glossary

AWL

A sharp, pointed marking tool. Often used to start screw holes.

BACK OR TENON SAW

A saw used for small work on the bench top. Usually no more than 10 inches (250mm) long.

BATTEN

Thin strips of any type of wood between ½ inch (12mm) and 1 inch (25mm) thick. May be flexible.

BEVEL

Woodworker's term for an angle, whether it's on a piece of lumber or it's the angled edge of a chisel or plane blade.

BUTT JOINT

Two flat facets of mating parts that fit flush together with no interlocking joinery.

CHAMFERING

Planing or cutting the square edge off finished work to produce an angle, often at 45 degrees.

CLAMP OR CRAMP

A tool that holds pieces of wood or other items together. Particularly useful for holding wood in place when gluing and assembling.

COMBINATION SQUARE

An all-metal, engineer's style square that can be used to mark up and check both 90 and 45 degree angles. The straight edge slides in and out.

COUNTERBORE

A straight-sided drilled hole that recesses a screw head below the wood's surface, so a wood plug can cover it. A counterboring bit combines a drill bit with a counterboring bit.

COUNTERSINK

A cone-shaped drilled hole that matches the sloped angle of the underside of a screw head and sinks it flush with the wood's surface. Also refers to the tool that makes this hole.

DOWEL

A round wooden pin or peg used in constructing joints.

GABLE

The vertical, triangular end of a roof.

HALVING JOINT

A joint formed by interlocking two pieces of lumber at an angle to each other. The pieces fit into housings that are cut half the thinckness of each piece of lumber.

HARDWOOD

Lumber from broad-leaved deciduous trees, no matter how dense it is. (Balsa is a hardwood.)

JIGSAW

A power saw with a short, thin blade. Ideal for cutting curves. Excellent first power tool to complement an electric drill.

MITER

The joining of wood by cutting it at an evenly-divided angle—usually 45 degrees.

MORTISE AND TENON JOINT

Means of connecting two pieces of wood, by cutting a square or rectangular hole (the mortise) in one piece that will accept a matching tongue (the tenon) in the other.

PILOT HOLE

A small drilled hole, used as a guide and pressure relief for screw insertion, or to locate additional drilling work such as counterboring and countersinking.

PLUG

Circular piece of wood that can be used to hide a screw head instead of using filler.

RIPPING

Sawing down the length of a board, with the grain.

SOFTWOOD

Lumber from coniferous trees. Most softwoods are pale, soft and resinous, but yew is hard and dark.

SPADE (OR FLAT) BIT

A drill bit made from a flat piece of steel designed to drill holes larger than holes drilled by standard twist drill bits.

T-SQUARE

A woodworker's testing device to ensure exact 90 degree angles.

Index

Credits

Quarto would like to thank and acknowledge the following for supplying pictures to be reproduced in this book:

(Key: l left, r right, c center, t top, b bottom)

COMPANY	DETAILS	PAGES
R.K. Alliston	+44 (0)845 130 5577 www.rkalliston.com	130bl, 132tr, 147tl
Allweather & Tubbs	+44 (0)1372 466106 www.allweatherandtubbs.co.uk	28 cl (lead chest), 30, 33tl, 33cl, 34bl, 34br, 35t, 36bl, 53br, 56bl, 56bc, 56br, 58bl, 59br, 100, 104bl, 104bc, 104r, 106tr, 107b
Barlow Tyrie Ltd	+44 (0)1376 557600 www.teak.com	28cl, 29br, 32tr, 54l, 54tr, 57tr, 57cr, 57br, 59tr, 60l, 60tr, 61r, 146l, 147bl
Bill Brown Bags Ltd	+44 (0)1403 255288 www.bill-brown.com	53r, 58br, 147tr
Bradshaw Direct Ltd	+44 (0)1904 691169 www.bradshawsdirect.co.uk	151tr
Childlife Play Systems	(photograph courtesy of Walpole Woodworkers) +1 800 467 9464 www.childlife.com	149br
CORBIS / Kim Robbie		149c
Country Casual	+1 800 284 8325 www.countrycasual.com	32l, 60br
Duncraft, Inc	+1 800 593 5656 www.duncraft.com	127tl, 128l, 128r, 129bl, 129tr, 129br, 130tr, 131bl, 131br, 133c, 133r
Erikson Birdhouse Co	+1 800 382 2473 www.bird-houses.com	127b
Forsham Cottage Arts	+44 (0)1233 820229 www.forshamcottagearks.com	126, 129c, 130br, 132br
GARDEN PICTURE LIBRARY / John Glover		105r
GARDEN PICTURE LIBRARY / Mel Watson		105l
The Garden Shop	+44 (0)870 7770099 www.thegardenshop.co.uk	150bl
Gwyn Carless Designs Ltd	www.gcdesigns.co.uk	151bl
Heritage Farms	+1 800 845 2473 www.heritagefarms.biz	131tr
The Heveningham Collection Ltd	+44 (0)1962 761777 www.heveningham.co.uk	34tl, 56t, 108br
J+G Garden Stone	+86 21 5031 7155 www.jggarden.com	33br
Lilliput Play Homes	(photograph courtesy of Walpole Woodworkers) +1 724 348 7071 www.lilliputplayhomes.com	149bl
Lloyd Christie	+44 (0)20 7351 2108 www.lloydchristie.com	57bc
Old Time Wheelbarrow Co	+1 604 855 1375 www.oldtimewheelbarrow.com	36br
Patio Furniture	+44 (0)1726 833366 www.patio-furniture.co.uk	150tr
Pots and Pithoi	+44 (0)1342 714793 www.pots-and-pithoi.co.uk	33tr
Rayment Wirework	+44 (0)1843 821628 www.raymentwire.co.uk	57tl
Riverside Plastics, Inc	+1 800 493 4945 www.riverside-plastics.com	35b
Stonebank Ironcraft Ltd	+44 (0)1285 720737 www.stonebank-ironcraft.co.uk	104tl
Teak Tiger	+44 (0)800 0680333 www.teaktigertrading.co.uk	52, 57bl, 58c, 59cr, 60cr, 61l, 150tl, 150br
TreeHouse Company	Design and Construction Specialists +44 (0)1560 600111 www.treehouse-company.com	148br
Tree Tops Play Equipment	+44 (0)1227 761899 www.treetopsdirect.co.uk	149t
Trellis Structures	+1 888 285 4624 www.trellisstructures.com	29cl, 102l, 106tl, 108bl, 109tl, 109tr
Walpole Woodworkers	+1 800 343 6948 www.walpolewoodworkers.com	32br, 33bl, 36t, 37tl, 37tr, 55bl, 102r, 103bl, 103br, 106b, 107t, 108tr, 109b, 127b, 130tl, 131tl, 131cl, 132bl, 133l, 145r, 146r, 148bl, 148tl, 148tr, 151br
Westminster Teak	+44 (0)1825 764222 www.westminsterteak.co.uk	28 cr (bench), 54br, 55tr, 55br, 58tl, 59bl, 144, 147br, 151tl
Wood Classics	+1 800 385 0030 www.woodclassics.com	28tr (pergola), 55tl, 101r, 103t

Quarto would like to thank and acknowledge **Toddington Garden Centre** and **Robert Young Flowers & Gifts** in Cheltenham, England, for lending plants for the finished shots.

Quarto would also like to thank and acknowledge **The McKergows, Carol Cowlishaw, Camilla and Jacob Pot** and **Jean Evans** for granting permission to photograph their gardens.

All other photographs and illustrations are the copyright of Quarto Publishing plc. While every effort has been made to credit contributors, Quarto would like to apologize for any unintended omissions or any errors.